MEET YOURSELF ON SUNDAY

Meet Yourself
ON SUNDAY

By

MASS OBSERVATION

with drawings by

RONALD SEARLE

This edition first published in 2009
by Faber and Faber Ltd
Bloomsbury House, 74–77 Great Russell Street
London WC1B 3DA

Printed by Books on Demand GmbH, Norderstedt

All rights reserved
© Mass Observation Archive, 1949
Illustrations © Ronald Searle, 1949

The right of Mass Observation Archive to be identified as author of this work
has been asserted in accordance with Section 77 of the
Copyright, Designs and Patents Act 1988

The right of Ronald Searle to be identified as illustrator of this work
has been asserted in accordance with Section 77 of the
Copyright, Designs and Patents Act 1988

This book is sold subject to the condition that it shall not, by way of
trade or otherwise, be lent, resold, hired out or otherwise circulated
without the publisher's prior consent in any form of binding or cover other than
that in which it is published and without a similar condition including this
condition being imposed on the subsequent purchaser

A CIP record for this book is available from the British Library

ISBN 978–0–571–25108–7

Our authorised representative in the EU for product safety is
Easy Access System Europe, Mustamäe tee 50, 10621 Tallinn, Estonia
gpsr.requests@easproject.com

Acknowledgments

In addition to the various authors and publications referred to in the footnotes to the text, Mass-Observation wishes to thank the following for their co-operation in this book: *The London Transport Executive; The Lord's Day Observance Society; The Youth Hostels Association; The British Institute of Public Opinion*, for permission to quote figures from surveys undertaken by them; The *Daily Graphic* for permission to quote from the findings of a survey by Mass-Observation, originally commissioned by that paper; and *George G. Harrap & Co. Ltd.*, for permission to use part of a Mass-Observation report which originally appeared in 'Exmoor Village'.

CONTENTS

Chapter		Page
I	SUNDAY MORNING FEELING	5
II	SUNDAY PAVEMENTS	14
III	SUNDAY IN A LONDON BOROUGH	19
IV	COUNTRY SUNDAY	25
V	SUNDAY IN WORKTOWN	31
VI	SABBATH INTO SUNDAY	33
VII	BRIGHT SPOTS	40
VIII	SUNDAY EXCURSION	46
IX	SUNDAY JAIL	53
X	THOUGHTS BEHIND LOCKED DOORS	55
XI	SABBATH SURVIVALS	63
XII	SUNDAY FANTASY	66
XIII	STAGGERING SUNDAY	71

CHAPTER I

SUNDAY MORNING FEELING

'Sunday morning feeling,
Not a thing to do,
We can't get special tickets to admit us to the Zoo.
So shall we do the crossword?
Or take a bus to Kew?
It's Sunday in London to-day.
Sitting by the fireside,
In an easy chair,
There's scandal in the papers and there's Handel
  on the air,
Salvation Army trumpets are blowing in the
  Square,
It's Sunday in London to-day.
There's nobody in the Strand,
And even Piccadilly looks deserted for the day,
But please don't misunderstand,
It may seem rather funny,
But we like it that way.
No one brings the letters,
No one brings the bread,
The pictures haven't opened,
So what shall we do instead?
We ought to call on father,
But let's go back to bed,
It's Sunday in London to-day.'*

THE 'SUNDAY MORNING FEELING' had made so strong an impression on the authors of this ditty that they wrote it whilst prisoners-of-war in Changi Gaol, Singapore. Two continents away from Piccadilly, they were not out of touch with Sunday mornings in London. Mass-Observation of Sunday habits makes it clear that most people do, in fact, spend not only Sunday morning but the entire day either in or around the home. Sunday gen-

Composer, Bill Williams. Author, Rawle Knox.

erally emerges as a day for aimlessness – often pleasant, as this book will show, but also, as in the song, often reluctant, restless and dull.

What do people do on Sunday whilst they are at home? Easily the most frequent pastime is the radio. Gallup Poll results, combining figures for summer and winter, show that as many as three-quarters of the population say they listen to the wireless on Sundays.* In addition, one in four stays in bed late, two in five visit or entertain, and one in six works in his garden or allotment. Away-from-home activities are much fewer. Two people in five go for a walk, one in six drinks at the pub, one in six is at work, one in seven goes to church, one in twelve goes to the cinema, and one in seven goes motoring. Expressed rather differently, it is roughly true to say that *out of every twenty people* in the population:

> 14 listen to the radio on Sundays
> 8 visit or entertain
> 8 go for a walk
> 4 garden
> 4 visit a pub
> 4 are at work
> 3 go to church
> 3 go motoring, etc.
> 2 go to the cinema

and most people do at least two of these things.

But statistics are dead representatives of live people, people who are best left to speak for themselves. First of all, the family man, chatting with his family, resting, pottering, with a break for the pub:

> 'I get up and have breakfast and go out in the garden and chop the wood – then I peel the potatoes and read the paper for a bit, then sit down and have my dinner. I always make it a practice to wash up and then I go and have a little nap for a couple of hours, coming down in time for tea. We sit down and have a chinwag – have about half-an-hour playing "spoof" – then me and my cripple boy go out and have a couple of wines, then we have another chinwag and it's time for bed – that's my day.' Ex-policeman, 60.

* *But not, of course, necessarily exclusive of any other occupation. The average person mentioned two or three things that he did on Sunday.*

SUNDAY MORNING FEELING

Sunday in a bed-sitting room for the single girl :

'Well, I share a bed-sitting room with a girl friend, and we get up late, about 10. Then we clean the room, cook lunch, then sit and read the newspapers and write letters. Then after tea we play cards with my friend's fiance when he comes around.'

Shorthand typist, 25.

The single man – friends and the radio:

'Oh, I stay in bed later, and sometimes I go into the works —otherwise I potter round my flat before lunch. I usually have a friend round to lunch and we go for a walk by the river in the afternoon. In the evening I go and see friends or sit at home and read or listen to the wireless.'

And the housewife, busiest member of the family:

'I usually get up and get breakfast, prepare the dinner, and do a bit of cleaning up. I don't get much sit-down, but look at the paper, maybe for half-an-hour, then get ready for tea-time and in the evening write letters or play a game of cards —I know it's naughty, but you've got to do something to pass the time. Summer evenings we go out for a stroll. Dad goes to the local and has a pint.'

Old Age Pensioner's wife, 66.

Asking people how they spend Sundays is one way of finding out what they do; another, in some respects more likely to give a true picture, is to watch them whilst they are unaware that they are observed. Here is just such an account of the routine of Sunday, gardening in a middle-class suburban neighbourhood:

By 7-45 on Sunday morning, the A..s are already inspecting their garden which they took over a year ago as an absolute shambles and have turned into an admirable garden. This, however, has taken much time, and Mr A... usually works for at least two hours in it every evening plus half day Saturday and all day Sunday.

Before 8-00 both Mr A... and wife are at work taking insects off plants. A brief break for breakfast and then he cuts front hedge and hoes side passage for weeds, etc. while wife plants new flowers. By 11 both are working on collecting stones to make a new path. At about 11-30 wife goes in to prepare dinner.

Dinner takes about half-an-hour and at about 1-30 they come out and have tea on the lawn. This now takes perhaps an hour and they may read the paper, but earlier in the year they usually started work within a few minutes of finishing.

Afternoon until tea-time is taken up with both spraying all the vegetables, weeding, hoeing, etc.

Tea in the garden and after tea (Sunday being the day that watering is legal) they start watering. This takes at least two hours on a garden that is probably 60 feet by 15. Every inch is soaked and resoaked. After this they walk slowly round the garden inspecting each flower. They go in at about 8 and usually are in bed shortly after 9.

Monday morning at about 8 they were already out inspecting the garden.

For the enthusiastic gardener there is plenty to do on Sundays. The father of small children, on the other hand, may find it next to impossible to achieve anything at all:

Mr B... intended to spend Sunday afternoon reading in the garden and an early meal was laid on for this purpose (wife wanted to do so as well). There was a deck chair in the shade and in the early afternoon B... started to read through all Sunday papers (four of them).

Four-year-old son had been playing with one-year-old daughter but wanted father to play with him as soon as B... came into the garden. B... refused saying that he wanted to read the paper. Boy carried on playing but then started asking questions, which B... answered. Then came up behind chair and started pulling B...'s hair. This gave him an idea and he started going through the motions of giving B...'s hair a shampoo, rubbing and ruffling the hair.

B... had no objections and went on reading. Boy then had further bright idea of using real water for shampoo, ran inside and found an old scent bottle that let water out a drip at a time. When entire bottle full was emptied drip by drip on B...'s hair, counter measures were necessary and B... started reaching behind him (still reading) and trying to catch boy. This was the beginning of a game which went on in this way for some time. Then boy saw the advantage of something bigger, dropped his bottle and fetched his toy watering-can, full of water from a bath that was on the lawn.

After a shower from this B... saw drastic action was necessary and chased the boy. Caught him and carried him to

SUNDAY MORNING FEELING

bath intending to put his head in. But as he lent over bath, wife came up from behind having picked up watering-can and emptied entire contents over B...'s head. Shrieks of laughter, lots of horseplay with the towel, and rest of afternoon spent floating boats on the bath. Papers did not get read until after the nine o'clock news.

A third report spotlights Sunday in a working-class household:

The family has three members: Stella, married (husband away in the Army), 24 years old, living on her husband's Army allowance; her two-year-old son, Steven; and her sister, Joan, 22, ex-ATS, at present clerk in a London office (described as 'friendly, pleasant disposition, but does little to help her sister with the housework'). The three live together in an old-fashioned flat in a South London suburb, part of which is sublet to a young married couple. This is how they spent their day, on Sunday in January:

8-45. Stella gets up. Comes into kitchen in pyjamas and dressing gown. Selects two cups and saucers from a pile of dirty crockery, washes them up, makes a pot of tea, takes tray into bedroom with *Sunday Pictorial*. They talk until 9-30.

9-30. Stella comes into kitchen again in pyjamas and dressing-gown. Starts to cook fritters and fried bread, goes to fetch Steven, gives him some of the cooked food in his hand, washes up two plates, and puts rest of food under grill to keep warm.

10-0. Makes another pot of tea. Stands drinking it and reading the paper. The dog is given some fish. Steven plays contentedly.

10-30. Joan gets up, goes to bathroom for quick wash, comes out into kitchen in pyjamas and dressing-gown. They eat at table the fritters and fried bread which have been kept warm nearly an hour.

11-0. Steven is washed, clean socks put on. Stella puts on her clothes. She washes up the crockery and tidies up the kitchen whilst Joan, in slacks and jumper, makes herself up in front of the kitchen mirror. The wireless still provides background music. Steven happy playing. Conversation centres mainly on clothes.

12-30. Joan washing underclothes in bathroom, Steven watching. Stella preparing pudding for dinner. Work is interrupted when other tenant makes cup of tea for all.

MEET YOURSELF ON SUNDAY

1-0. Stella cooking, Steven playing, Joan plucking eyebrows in front of kitchen mirror. The two women talking about artists heard at the moment on 'Family Favourites'.

2-0. All have dinner. Steven sitting up in high chair, meat cut up for him in small pieces. Menu: joint, boiled potatoes, sprouts, suet pudding with golden syrup – pot of tea. Wireless background.

3-0. Stella washes and wipes up dinner things – then joins Joan, playing with Steven. They talk. Joan makes a pot of tea.

3-30 to 6-0. Both women sitting in front of kitchen fire quietly reading. Stella *Red Star Weekly*, *Women's Own* and *Sunday Pictorial* – Joan, *American Comics*. Steven plays with cards. Dog asleep. Wireless background – light programme. Bursts of conversation – bursts of knitting.

6-0. Stella laying tea, bread and butter, jam, jam sponge, pot of tea in kitchen.

7-0. Joan has been down to see Uncle and Aunt downstairs; now back in the kitchen, reading a pile of *Woman* magazines. A fresh pot of tea has been made and Stella is putting Steven to bed in his cot. (Just before 7-0 he had a quick wash).

8-0 to 10-0. Like the afternoon again. Both women reading: Joan *The Woman* – Stella *News of the World* borrowed from downstairs (Uncle and Aunt). Wireless background. Bursts of knitting, talking, laughing, humming to the wireless which is on all the time.

10-30. Sitting over supper – talking about underwear. Stella writes a letter to her husband. Joan writes a letter too.

11-30. Library books open (novels) but both talking. Stella begins to tie up hair. The dog is sent down the garden for a few minutes.

12-30. They go to bed.

This is possibly not a typical family, but the pattern of Sunday – spent in a mildly pleasant, aimless sort of way – is the customary one, as well as the tendency to spend the entire day at home. Moreover this diary is interesting as an illustration of the way in which the Sunday output of effort is often largely confined to catching up on odd jobs, and to cooking and eating the Sunday dinner. Food is a big item in Sunday at home, and the high-

spot of Sunday food is dinner. Recently Mass-Observation asked its National Panel of Voluntary Observers* to keep an account of their meals on a Wednesday and a Sunday of November, 1948. Results showed that meals, for the middle-class at least, are bigger and better on Sundays:

> The best rations are reserved for Sunday – on that day twice as many people have eggs for breakfast as on Wednesday, and bacon, sausages and ham play a more important part, but very little fish. Lunch offers for the most part the

*A largely middle-class group of people who every month send long, detailed replies to questions on their habits and attitudes; questions concern a wide variety of subjects, ranging from party games to world organisation. The Mass-Observation Monthly Bulletin publishes some of the results, this one being released in January, 1949.

fullest variety, and with large helpings at that. Soup is the exception rather than the rule, but very few people go without rationed meat – what one man calls the 'Sunday joint and accessories' is an established institution. It usually takes the form of lamb or mutton or roast beef and it is always accompanied by a quite formidable array of vegetables. Besides potatoes in various styles, there is Yorkshire pudding, if there is beef, and two or more other vegetables – dried or tinned peas, cauliflower, brussel sprouts and cabbage being the most popular. With mutton, jelly is frequently mentioned, and the finishing touch is given by the gravy and often a mint sauce. There are the same varieties of dessert as on Wednesdays, and again as on Wednesdays tea and coffee vie closely for popularity after the meal. During it there is sometimes quite a variety of other drinks, such as mineral waters, lemonade, cider, beer, which rarely appear on Wednesday's menu. This is a typical Sunday lunch, as eaten by the family of a 33-year old housewife:

Roast mutton, roast potatoes, sprouts, dried peas, gravy, guava jelly (U.S.A. gift), chocolate blancmange, grape tart.

Afternoon tea is on the whole a more weighty meal than on Wednesday, more people eating more bread, more jam, more fruit, and especially – more cakes. 'Green' teas are also popular on Sunday. There are fewer full-suppers, but twice as many light ones as on Wednesday. While high teas are often very elaborate with several kinds of bread and cake and buns and biscuits, as well as jelly or fruit. This is a typical Sunday High Tea:

Tinned grapes, jelly and custard, snoek and tomatoes, cakes and sponge cakes – tea.

The Bed-time Snack follows the same simple lines as on weekdays. (Milk drinks, bread and cheese, or biscuits).

The report concludes that 'Sunday is still clearly an excuse for solid stuffing.' The Sunday stuffing is not confined to food. *The Sunday newspaper* provides an opportunity for an equally solid intake of feature articles, serial stories, sports news, gossip and scandal, and to a lesser extent, serious news too. A recent national survey * outlining the extent to which every kind of newspaper is read, showed that *more* people read *more* newspapers on

*'*The Hulton Readership Survey*, 1948'

SUNDAY MORNING FEELING

Sundays than weekdays. During the week, although most people read a daily paper, only a minority (23 per cent.) take more than one. On Sunday the picture is different. Out of every one hundred people in England and Wales:

> 26 read three or more Sunday papers
> 36 read two
> 30 read one
> and only 8 read none at all.

Moreover, Sunday newspaper reading differs from that of weekdays in kind as well as extent. A survey made by Mass-Observation in 1947-48 showed that the newspaper reader more or less assumes a different personality on Sunday, a day when every second person reads the *News of the World*. In general, the Sunday orgy of newspaper reading leads people to look for features and feature articles, as well as to concentrate on news that is exclusive and entertaining, and with the emphasis nicely planted on gossip and scandal.

This is Sunday at home, reading the *News of the World*, eating solid meals, getting up late, aimlessly pottering. A later chapter will show how people feel about Sundays spent in this way, how far the slow tempo is a mark of real contentment, how far of reluctant leisure. But first, Sunday out of doors ...

CHAPTER II
SUNDAY PAVEMENTS

EVEN TO Charles Lamb, over one hundred years ago, when Sunday was still the Sabbath, retaining much more of its religious value than it has to-day, seen from the street it still seemed a day of gloom and emptiness:

> 'There is a gloom for me attendant upon a city Sunday, a weight in the air. I miss the cheerful cries of London – the music and the ballad-singer – the buzz and stirring murmur of the streets. Those eternal bells depress me. The closed shops repel me. Prints, pictures, all the glittering and endless succession of knacks and gewgaws, and ostentatiously displayed wares of tradesmen, which make a weekday saunter through the less busy parts of the metropolis so delightful – are shut out. No bookstalls deliciously to idle over – no busy faces to recreate the idle man who contemplates them ever passing by – nothing to be seen but unhappy countenances – or half-happy at best...the very strollers in the fields on that day look anything but comfortable.'
>
> Charles Lamb: *The Essays of Elia*, 1823.

One of the chief similarities between Sunday to-day and Sunday a century ago, is that, from the outside at least, both give the same impression of emptiness. Although *in the home* most people now feel themselves free to do much as they please on Sundays, restrictions have not been correspondingly lifted from public places. In Scottish parks even to-day, children's swings are put out of use on Sundays, and in London, black spot to Sabbatarians:

Theatres are closed (except to club-members).
Dance halls are closed (except for club-members).
Pubs have shorter opening hours.
Most shops are closed.
Most cafes and restaurants are closed.
Museums and exhibitions have shorter hours, or are closed.
Cinemas have shorter hours.
Most games of organised sport are illegal.
Transport starts late and is less frequent.

SUNDAY PAVEMENTS

Libraries are shut.

There is no postal delivery.

Even though, on the whole, people are now mildly prepared to *enjoy* Sunday in a non-religious fashion, the increase in outside facilities for enjoyment has not kept pace with the change in popular attitude. Sunday has become, perforce, a home and family day – and out-of-doors, in winter at least, the scene is not much more cheerful than it appeared to Lamb in 1823. Sunday in the West End, for instance:

> Piccadilly, mid-day Sunday. Pavements are empty except for a few strollers, who look like Londoners taking a casual walk in familiar surroundings. Not till shortly after four o'clock do large numbers start to come from subways and buses to join the Leicester Square picture queues. An hour or two later, parties of four or five youths begin to appear, swaggering in best Sunday clothes – with an eye (for the most part unsuccessfully) for any female below forty...

A street photographer, interviewed at his job in Trafalgar Square, gave a rather brighter picture of central London sightseeing:

> 'Sunday is the Londoner's day, that's when he likes to come out and have a look around the Square. He comes on Saturday too – but not like on Sundays. You get him on Sunday with his wife and kids, looking at the lions and the fountains – now they've got the fountains going. Yes, it stands to reason Sunday's our best day – he comes out with money in his pocket and he doesn't mind spending a little. He's a different man on Sunday, because that's when he's got his family with him and he likes to look around. Rain or shine, there's always a lot comes out on a Sunday...'

But, on the whole, apart from its sightseeing functions, the keynote to the central London week-end is aimlessness. Moreover, the Sunday atmosphere is so pervasive that it affects even those to whom the religious and holiday values of the day are nothing. A Soho *habitué* for instance, reported for us on Sunday in Soho; it is a good account of the way in which the cheerless atmosphere of the Soho streets on Sunday drives people into their houses, and envelops them even there:

> 'In the part of Soho that I frequent, Sunday is regarded as a dull and miserable day. At least, it is by the people who

SUNDAY PAVEMENTS

have ever mentioned it to me. I never go out at all on Sundays if I can avoid it. I have occasionally wondered why I have this habit of staying indoors on Sunday – and I really don't know the answer. There is certainly no personal religious connection, though I may be influenced subconsciously by the general atmosphere of Sunday, which, of course, comes from the religious idea. My father was an agnostic and ignored the religious side of Sunday altogether. My mother, who was "nothing at all" in the religious sense and never went to Church, regarded Sunday as a day of rest because she had a grocery shop and worked hard all the week. I suppose it must be the influence of those childhood Sundays that has affected me ever since. I still cling to the idea of peace, a bright fire, and hours of reading.

'The people I know who frequent the cafes and pubs of my particular bit of Soho, are mostly small time crooks, gamblers, prostitutes and continentals, who do not work and who have no interest in religion now, whatever their backgrounds may have been. So there is no obvious reason why Sunday should be any different to them than any other day. The cafes are open (not all), the cinemas and the pubs, and still I have frequently heard them saying, "Oh – I hate Sunday" – "Sunday is a miserable day," etc. The only reasons I've heard them give are, "Well, there's nobody around," and "You can't get cigarettes." The cigarette question must have only arisen in recent years, because, presumably at one time, they would buy several packets on Saturday to last till Monday. But now it is a great problem, everybody runs short; shops are closed, pubs and cafes have very few, if any, and everybody tries to borrow off everyone else, so that even if one has a spare packet, he very soon has to part with it. But why should "nobody be around"? Actually there are only about half the usual daily customers in the cafes and pubs, but why do they stay away ? Perhaps some, a very few, have wives and homes, and are expected to stay home on Sundays. But the ones I know of live in furnished rooms or hostels or nowhere at all particularly, so why do they stay away from their usual haunts on Sunday ? If you asked them, they would say "Because Sunday is so miserable – there's nobody around" – so there you are – a vicious circle. Some just stay in bed all day – others go and listen to the speakers in

MEET YOURSELF ON SUNDAY

Hyde Park (which they never do in the week), and then go to the pictures. I had a man friend once who shared my flat for some years. All that time he did not work – he just spent his whole day and evening, sitting in one cafe or another, going to the cinemas, or occasionally walking round the West End. But he, too, hated Sunday, and finally got so bored with going around Soho on Sunday that he took to sharing my quiet Sunday by the fire, although he was a man who hated to stay in the house at all. With regard to the gamblers, those who play cards and dice, etc. they gamble just the same on Sundays, if there is a game going, but they too, dislike Sunday. Of course, the "dog" and "horse" gamblers will miss these things on Sundays, but then there are not dog and horse races every day in the week. And the drinkers will probably have been more drunk than usual on Saturday and spent their money, so will naturally feel flat and miserable on Sunday ; but why should they get drunk particularly on Saturday and not on Sunday, if they don't work during the week ? Simply, I presume, because of the prevailing atmosphere – "Everybody" goes gay on Saturday, "everybody" is more quiet and dull on Sunday.'

In other words, central London Sunday is, broadly speaking, a hangover. Much the same is true of Sunday in the upper middle class district of South Kensington, a residential district, where people tend either to stay indoors or go elsewhere on Sundays. Counts of passers-by both at mid-day and in early evening showed twice as many people about on Saturdays as on Sundays.

Sunday lunch-time in the South Kensington district boasted three cafes open (very crowded) in place of the eighteen available on Saturday and Monday. But the museum centre, Exhibition Road, was at its busiest on Sunday:

> More crowded than on Saturday or Monday, many people in groups of four or five. A small queue outside the Science Museum, together with ice-cream salesman and a fruit barrow.

Whilst in purely residential streets there was the familiar Sunday emptiness:

> Residential streets practically deserted. After 6-0 quite a few dressed up old ladies looking as if they would be going to Church. Nobody hurrying.

CHAPTER III

SUNDAY IN A LONDON BOROUGH

THESE ARE the Sundays of central London: Soho, Piccadilly, and Kensington. But most people stay more or less at home on Sunday – and for the bulk of London's 8,000,000, home is the suburb rather than the city. One in every eighty of all Londoners, for instance, live in the Borough of Hammersmith, a working class, Labour area, fifteen minutes on the Underground from Piccadilly Circus, but closely-knit in spite of its proximity to the West End.

What facilities, apart from religious ones, does Hammersmith – a 'go-ahead' Borough – provide on Sundays for its residents? An interview with the newly-appointed Entertainments Officer, produced the following list of officially recognised Sunday facilities:

    a. Indoor swimming baths – open Sunday mornings.
    b. Tennis Courts.
    c. Use of football pitches.
    d. Youth Club open on Sunday.
    e. Private rowing clubs.
    f. Two cinemas running Sunday films and concerts.
    g. Two theatres running Sunday Theatre Clubs.
    h. Monthly concerts.
    i. Private club running concerts, mostly variety.
    j. Musical Society, Gramophone and Dramatic Club, Church-attached.
    k. Sunday Dance Club – Palais-de-Dance.

This is more than most districts have to offer on Sundays, but not a lot to cater for over 100,000 people. In addition, there are, of course, churches and pubs, but only one person in seven goes to church, and in Southern England only one in nine. Sunday pub-going on the other hand, habitual to one person in every six in the country as a whole, is more frequent in the South. Here is one investigator's report on Sunday evening (7-45 p.m.) in a small working-class pub in the centre of Hammersmith:

MEET YOURSELF ON SUNDAY

'The private bar (mixed) is the smallest of the pub's three rooms. None of the bars are quite so crowded as last night. Fourteen people present in the private bar, all unskilled working class. Three women and eleven men, equal numbers over and under forty. Equal numbers in best clothes and ordinary clothes. Only one, a middle-aged woman, was here last night. A piano accordion plays Irish medleys at the public bar door. A man on crutches goes through all the bars collecting money in a hat: five men in the private bar contribute coppers.'

Hardly a scene of Sunday dissipation, although – except for Saturday – considerably brighter than during the week.* Past Mass-Observation surveys on pubs and drinking have shown that Saturday is the peak night for the pub, with a slight drop on Sundays and Fridays, and a lower attendance level for the rest of the week. But drunkenness is no more frequent on Sundays than week-days, and less frequent than on Saturdays, largely because at week-ends people drink more slowly; aimlessness is again the Sunday key-note, even in the pub. A relatively quiet way of spending Sunday, the pub is still for some people – like this elderly night watchman – more or less the only way:

'I generally have a sleep, then I go in the pub. Then I go home to dinner and then have another sleep. When you get old the pub is like a club – we old 'uns don't want to roam the streets.'

Night Watchman, 62 – Hammersmith.

For the older working people there is *no* Sunday alternative to pub, church, or, of course, to staying at home or 'roaming the streets.' And street roaming, amongst older people at least, is an activity for Saturday rather than Sunday. A clue to this is provided by the numbers of people leaning over the street safety railings in the centre of Hammersmith. On Saturday, in a late winter afternoon, one twenty-yard stretch was taken up by nineteen people, exclusively working men, mostly in their working clothes, and mostly middle-aged or elderly. Some read the evening paper, more just watched the crowds go by. But on Sunday at the same time the line of old men had thinned to a few young ones. There

As in almost all our observational work for this survey, the same pub was observed at the same time on Saturday, Sunday and Monday.

SUNDAY IN A LONDON BOROUGH

were only *four* people leaning on this part of the rails; and each of these was under forty.

Most of our material supports the view that older men tend to spend Sunday either at home or in the pub.

The street and the cinema are noticeably both patronised by the young rather than the old. The Hammersmith Palais-de-Danse, open on Sunday to club members, is largely an affair of the under-thirties. Sunday park-strollers are younger on Sundays than on week-days, and only in the large-scale whist drive that takes place regularly in the centre of Hammersmith did we find a predominance of older people of the working classes.

Youth has rather more to attract it on Sundays, although not a lot. Besides the Dance-hall and the cinema, there is, for instance,

MEET YOURSELF ON SUNDAY

in Hammersmith, the spontaneous self-organised entertainment of strictly amateur 'speedway' racing (on bicycles) that takes place on Sunday afternoons. An investigator reports:

'Opposite Ravenscourt Park entrance is a piece of level waste ground, the site of four or five bombed houses; it has been covered with cinders. A circle of bricks and stones has been made, about 30 feet in diameter. On the outside of this circle, every other Sunday, two teams of twelve persons each race on old, battered, but suitably adapted bicycles. Ages of riders range from about 14 – 18 years, they are all boys. Apparently there are several teams in many parts of London, and two of them meet for a match either "home" or "away" every Sunday afternoon. On this particular Sunday "White City Racers" (Hammersmith) were having a home match with "W.R.W." (Wembley). All the arrangements for the matches are done by the boys themselves. They dress as much like speedway riders as possible—some wear crash-helmets, gaiters, steel-tipped boots or gum-boots. All wear a pseudo-leather body-covering on which is painted their club colours and club name. As in the Speedway, heats of four are run. The two teams, one stationed at each end of the track, send two representatives to the "tapes" – a rubber inner tube, tied to a stone, and stretched across the front wheels of the four cycles. The inner tube snaps back, and off they go, anti-clockwise round the track. The cycles have no mudguards or brakes, and when corners are reached riders skid round, their left foot on the ground, looking very much like the real thing. Spills and thrills are frequent, serious accidents very few. A fifty year old workman, who was watching, told the investigator that he had come along every other Sunday ever since he first noticed them six weeks ago. "It's a good sport, you see some good riders. Sometimes this side-street is packed with cars and cycles and people, crowds come to watch them sometimes." On this particular Sunday afternoon about twenty people were watching, mostly youths of both sexes.'

Here is a sport got up by youth, for themselves, by themselves, for their amusement on Sundays. At the opposite extreme is the amusement arcade, centre of attraction for the more aimless type of working-class youth; two of these arcades are open in the centre of Hammersmith on Sunday afternoons, and both exhibit a

SUNDAY IN A LONDON BOROUGH

younger clientele on Sundays than week-days. An investigator describes the group lounging round the entrance to one:

> 'The boys have their hair done "spiv" fashion – swept upwards from the side-back; wear ready-made hand-stitched suits, too long and too broad at the shoulders. The girls have short skirts, tight-fitting costumes and are heavily made-up.'

The other arcade is smaller, and attracts a different type of Sunday custom:

> 'The smaller arcade seems to be a resting-room for a group of old age pensioners with nowhere to go. Very few dress "spiv" fashion here, it's mostly older men and young lads, all scruffily dressed.'

What else do people do on Sundays, in Hammersmith? Some stroll in their best clothes in the Park – for the most part in family groups. Couples make use of the tow-path for an afternoon riverside walk. Some sit in cafes and restaurants, about ¾ of which are usually open on Sundays. Lyons, in particular, forms a minor social centre on Sundays, *and this time for older people*, working-class. The Hammersmith branch of Lyons serves a special Sunday lunch, and many people sit on afterwards chatting across the tables, reading the paper, doing the crossword puzzle, long after they have finished their meal. One seventy-year-old labourer commented:

> 'They're people living in lodgings like myself. They've nowhere else to go – even the libraries are shut. It's better to have dinner here than in your lodgings – it makes a change and it's brighter. I like to sit and read my Sunday paper; it's a welcome change from my own room; it's generally warm here too. I can save my coal, and there's nowhere else to go...'

Tea time at Lyons is still a type of social club, but this time for the younger age-groups:

> '5 p.m. The place is packed with young people of all ages, teen-agers, young people in early and mid-twenties, young mothers, with children racing round the tables, and with ice-cream double or single. Occasionally mothers wave to each other at different tables. In ten minutes 64 people passed along the food counter, men and women in equal numbers, but rather more under forty than over.'

MEET YOURSELF ON SUNDAY

Finally, the street. An investigator made reports on a middle-class and a working-class street at the same time (early evening) on Saturday, Sunday and Monday. On no occasion was there much activity, but in both streets Sunday was the quietest of the three days:

'A working-class street in Hammersmith, early evening, Sunday.

'Very quiet, nobody about. The pub at the corner is shut. A dog sniffles into an alley nearby. A forty-year-old working man, dressed in his ordinary clothes, walks along and passes into a side street, hands in trouser pockets, sniffing as he walks along. A 55-year-old unskilled worker passes by in his best clothes, belching. A boy begins to sing in the house opposite. It is just possible to hear trains from the Metropolitan railway – the track runs parallel to this back street. A young unskilled worker, hands in pockets, eyes on his feet, shuffles into a side-street, whistling softly. An old working man turns into the side street opposite, after looking into the window of a closed general shop. The distant sound of a fire engine, and the radio from a house some way away. The light goes on upstairs in the house opposite. A group of youths go by, laughing and talking loudly. "I've only got fourpence" "Can't get a double gin with that" "Where did you say?" "*Where?*" '

CHAPTER IV
COUNTRY SUNDAY

SO MUCH FOR Sunday in winter, in London. Is it so very different out of town ? Our facts suggest that Sunday is much the same everywhere, a day to be spent for the most part in or around the home. Here, for instance, is the pattern of Sunday, seen from outside, in a Surrey village:

> 'The village is situated in Surrey on a busy main South coast road. During the week there is a steady stream of heavy lorries and commercial vehicles, but on this winter Sunday morning at 9 o'clock, the street is deserted. There is some movement around the paper shop. One small boy runs into the shop and reappears with a newspaper. The next customer

is a middle-aged man with a fawn muffler tucked into his coat. He walks briskly into the shop, buys his paper and then walks off down the road. No one loiters outside the shop, there is a cold north-easterly wind blowing.

'Up the high street and across the village green, all is quiet except for a sheep dog and a mongrel terrier romping together. Just outside the village in a field a tractor is chugging up and down in a zig-zag line pulling a truckload of kale. A farm worker stands on top of the kale throwing handfuls either side of the truck as fast as he can. The cattle, nosing the kale, follow the tractor and its load down the field. Asked about his Sunday habits a cowman said – "On Sundays I work same as any other day," and after a moment's thought added – "I sits down and eats my Sunday dinner. I'll tell you what the others are doing. They are lying on their beds reading the Sunday newspapers."

'The Church, lying on the far-side outskirts of the village, scarcely disturbs the picture. But at 3 o'clock there are more people about. A man, 35-40, wearing blue dungarees, a raincoat and fawn cloth cap, is slowly walking along holding the hand of a two-year-old child. A woman in a short brown fur coat, and hatless, pushes a small yellow perambulator. Three children – the oldest about seven – tidily dressed in black, fawn and grey overcoats, come out of the sweet shop with three ice cream cornets. Several houses already show lights, but curtains remain undrawn. Red, single deck buses are now plying up and down the road at fifteen minute intervals and average about four passengers. Cafes are open but empty although the tables are laid for tea, and in two of them fires are burning. The only place doing business – apart from the sweet shop – is the snack bar. Here a cluster of cycles are propped against the wall and two young cyclists are standing together. Two RAC motor cyclists stop outside the snack bar, park their vehicles and enter the cafe where it is warm, although there is no fire, and the counter is piled high with slices of currant cake and glossy buns. The two RAC riders order a cup of tea and bun and proceed to a table, where they unbutton their heavy overcoats and sit down rather stiffly. They give the impression of being well padded under their regulation coats. At another table two girls, aged about 17, are talking and laughing loudly together. They are dressed rather alike, with coloured scarves over their hair and three-quarter length coats.

'Round by the back of the High Street there is a slight change by now. Five lines of washing blow in the wind. A man 30-35, wearing grey slacks, grey hand-knitted pullover and carpet slippers, is sweeping his garden path. Two houses away another man, dressed in cloth cap and fawn raincoat, squats down, hammering in an iron rod beneath his window. The village green is empty. Back in the High Street an old local is ambling along smoking a pipe, leaning heavily on a stick...'

In summer the same village presents a very different picture. But even then people seldom venture very far from their homes except for an occasional break from routine such as the British Legion's annual outing to the South Coast. Here is the village at 7-30 on the June morning of that once-yearly occasion:

'Up the road come a string of eight green buses. They slow up, stop, then turn into a side street, followed by three men who have been waiting for them. After a time people begin to gather around. Two little boys come up first, aged about nine and six, both dressed alike, their fair hair neatly parted and brushed, and looking cool and clean. A plump woman walks by the side of her husband, holding the hand of a little boy who has to run to keep pace with them. She wears a floral silk dress, no stockings and beige sandals. Her husband, in a blue blazer, carries a basket covered with a white napkin, and the child holds a gaily painted bucket, with a picture of Mickey Mouse on the outside and inside a clean bright orange. They walk across to the buses where people are gathering. Young men in flannels, sports jackets and open-necked shirts, older men in lounge suits. All the men have button-holes and a few of the older ones carry walking sticks. Girls wear cotton or floral silk dresses, and most of the older women have straw or felt hats. All ages carry handbags; the large wide bulging black bag of the older woman: the much battered flap-over bag, tucked under the arm or resting on top of the basket, of the housewife, and the more complicated modern handbag of the young girl.

'A short stout woman climbs into the first bus, followed by another woman with two children, and they stand in the gangway of the coach looking at the seats. The children go to the long back seat, kneel on it and look at the bus and driver at the back. There is a burble of voices as the gathering increases. The buses fill up. Cases and parcels are pushed on the luggage racks. A little boy climbs into a bus behind his mother, holding a small butterfly net, and a jam jar suspended on a piece of string. He says, "Mum, let's sit at the back." She doesn't hear. He gives her the jam jar and net and goes to the back seat.

'At 8-15 the drivers climb into their cabins and start up the engines. It looks as though they are ready – fifteen minutes behind schedule. The passengers are smiling and talking and making themselves comfortable, jostling with the luggage on the racks, as the coaches move slowly out to the mainstreet.'

But even in summer it is seldom that the villagers go much further afield than the village green:

'At half-past three it is very hot. A cricket match is in progress, watched by men and women of all ages. Family groups are scattered on the outskirts of the green, sitting in the shade of the elms. A middle-aged man in flannels and sports jacket stands smoking a pipe and watching the match; a spaniel pants at his feet. On his right is a group of four, two boys and two girls – the boys sit following the play, but the girls show no interest in the game, instead they chat and giggle together, lying on the grass. Propped against the railings is a tandem cycle; the man, dressed in khaki shorts and white shirt sits on a seat absorbed in the game; the woman sits on the grass and knits, facing out into the road. Three or four children turn somersaults over the railings and pull each other about. Everyone looks extremely hot ...'

Towards the end of the day trippers and sight-seers themselves turn into an entertainment for the more leisurely watchful villagers:

'At 7-30 it is much cooler. The direction of traffic is now reversed, four-fifths of it going back to London. Cyclists pour through the village in squads of bare legs, white shirts and shorts; the local residents stand or sit in their gardens, loll against window-sills, hang over gates, or lean out of upstairs windows watching the traffic, which is going steadily; private and hired cars, coaches, cyclists, motor bikes; the

COUNTRY SUNDAY

pubs are open again, full and over-flowing outside with men and women drinking beer and soft drinks. Outside the cafes, pubs and sweetshops, the ground is littered with sweet and ice cream papers, empty cartons, paper bags, cigarette packets, match-boxes, debris of the day ...'

The heat-wave Sunday can provide attractions that Sunday in winter cannot begin to emulate. In summer time again an Observer describes Sunday in a village, where she had lived for some months, watching and mixing with the people:

'The village has been extremely quiet all day. No one out at 9 a.m. At 10 a.m. there were signs of life in the houses, but no one in the streets. The Church service on the BBC could be heard from Mrs T's house, and from Mrs K's. Mrs K says she always listens – can't go to church because of her leg. The villagers – that is the common general part of the village – did not go to church. Apart from children only Mrs T and two Miss P's represented this section at church. Nevertheless on leaving church one met no one in the street. Even Mrs G wasn't on her step. Mrs W was hanging out her washing; Mr H was fixing a deck chair in the back garden; Nancy S stood at her doorway; Mrs W had done quite a lot of washing. In the afternoon most of the men sat in their arm-chairs and had a sleep. At 2-30 Mr W was standing in his Sunday best gazing contemplatively at his vegetable garden. Mrs W was standing in a flowered apron at her side-door; two or three children were playing along the road; Tim H and his girl-friend Queenie were walking along together. Several families were sitting in their gardens in deck chairs – the R's and H's and others.

'A few people came out in the evening. At 6 p.m. several men were gathered at the K's doorstep. At 6-30 there was another church service. Young boys on bicycles cycled aimlessly up and down. One of the A's in particular was executing a cycling trick – cycling backwards in circles. Mr H and Mr W went to a neighbouring pub in the evening.

'At 7-30 Mrs A was gossiping with Mrs G outside her house. Mrs C, cloth cap on head, was working in her garden. At 9 p.m. there was no one down the street. At the corner by the shop, Mr K in his Sunday suit, with grey alpaca jacket, instead of brown one, was standing talking to the policeman.

Nancy S in a flowery green dress stood at the K's door, with Winifred S in her white flannel nightgown.

'At 9-30 p.m. Tim H cycled back from a visit to Queenie. Mr S in Sunday clothes – blue jacket, grey trousers, cloth cap – walked out from his house, followed by his collie-dog. He went over to his dairy to look at the cows. Mrs R, in pink flowered overalls over pink jumper, went into the S's house. Mr K went indoors. Mr M was standing outside his house playing with children, Basil H playing in his front garden.'

The observer summed up:

'Sunday remains a day of rest in the village, despite the lack of religious activity. Best clothes are worn, although frequently people don't go beyond their house and garden and the village street. But there is little feeling that work should not be done on Sundays. Women often do their washing; the men sometimes have to work on the land. But Sunday is the day when people take things easy, get up late, keep indoors or in the garden in the morning, and walk or gossip in the village street in the late afternoon or evening. That is the scene on a Sunday, resting, moving around slowly and locally.'

Nationally, churches, pubs and cinemas offer the only large-scale away-from-home Sunday opportunities and, in the village last described, none of these exist. In a Welsh-border mining village that has had long-term study, pubs are shut on Sundays, in accordance with Welsh custom, but there is a surge across the border for the nearest English beer. And in addition there is 'hole-in-the-corner' drinking; one landlord said:

'We don't open on Sundays, but in other pubs people will go round to the back door. You'd have people in your kitchen all day long if you once started.'

Whether it is pub or home, the normal village Sunday is spent very much round the 'back door.' Is it the same in the English provincial town?

CHAPTER V
SUNDAY IN WORKTOWN

REPORTS FROM the larger Northern towns present, superficially at least, a very similar picture of Sunday. Pubs are a major attraction – and in the summer, parks and the bus station; except for churches and cinema these provide more or less the only available facilities. Here is the pattern of a Sunday in 'Worktown', a large industrial city in the North:

'The town seems to look much cleaner on Sunday, probably because fewer people are about and these dressed in "best" Sunday clothes. Traffic is at a minimum. In the middle-class outskirts of the town church-goers, usually in family groups, wait for buses or walk towards the town centre where most of the churches are situated. Apart from these the only early morning passers-by are men in search of cigarettes or newspapers, going to the local newsagents or, because of the cigarette shortage, further afield, to the town centre. Church bells chime endlessly, from early morning till 11 o'clock. Except for churchgoers the town centre is more or less deserted until the pubs open, when men in search of a pint before dinner begin to arrive at the town-centre pubs. Women are rarely seen in the pubs on a Sunday mid-day, probably because they are too busy preparing Sunday dinner.

'At about 2-30 the afternoon procession of couples – family groups, youths and girls – begins to circulate round the middle of the town, window shopping, strolling, or on a fine day waiting for buses out to the country. And roundabout 3-30 queues begin to form outside the picture houses ready for the 4 o'clock opening ...

'Evening Church services seem to be poorly attended, but the pubs are very busy indeed; trade is mostly of a family character – Sunday evening is the one time in the week when men can be seen drinking with their wives ...

'In the town centre young men and girls hang round, lounging, picking up, back-chatting with each other. But

MEET YOURSELF ON SUNDAY

activity mostly ceases about 10 p.m.; last buses leave the centre of the town about that time, and after this there are few people about besides pub and cinema goers walking home to bed.'

In 'Steeltown', a Dock and Steelworks centre, the accent is again – in winter at least – on the pubs; reports suggest that people not only spend more time in pubs on Sundays than on week-days (except Saturday) but tend to behave in a different manner. The atmosphere of leisure and aimlessness percolating through into the pub makes drinking less of a business, more of a social occasion:

> A fifty year old Police Inspector comes into the bar every midday and drinks two or three halves of bitter – treating nobody and nobody treating him. There is a complete understanding on this matter. On a Sunday midday he has as many as nine halves of bitter – being treated, and, in his turn, buying rounds. This happens every Sunday lunch time. Not having to return to work, and free of his responsibility as a Police Officer, he lets himself go. Apart from evening sessions during the week, Sunday midday is the only time he is able to behave as he would like to in this bar.

Apart from cinemas and the Sunday recitals which occur about four times a year, usually with a rather poor attendance, Sundays in Steeltown provide little else to entice people out of their homes. But in summertime the city manages to present a rather brighter picture:

> The Bus station is packed and the buses on their way to the nearby vales and dales and seaside places are crowded. On the way out of the town they speed past queues waiting hopefully at request stops ...
>
> In the afternoon people surge into the park, all the boats are out on the lake, children play on the swings, the seats are full, and everywhere are men and women, children, couples, youths, lying around on the grass. But in winter it is quite different – people just don't come out of the house.

CHAPTER VI

SABBATH INTO SUNDAY

'Remember that thou keep holy the Sabbath Day. Six days shalt thou labour, and do all that thou hast to do, but the seventh day is the Sabbath of the Lord thy God.'
4th Commandment.

THE TWENTIETH CENTURY has seen 'the Lord's Day' – the religious 'Sabbath' of the 4th Commandment – stripped of the greater part of its earlier religious compulsions, dwindle into a vague shadow of its former self. It has become merely Sunday, to many people a relatively characterless day which rounds off Saturday rather than religiously initiating Monday and the week's work. To compensate for its loss of religious character, Sunday has not even gained much as a non-religious feast day; to a large extent it has grown into a day of negatives and emptiness.

But negatives were not always a feature of Sunday, even before Puritanism transformed it into the Jewish Sabbath. In Shakespeare's day, pre-Puritan, Sunday was a time for festival as well as church-going. According to Besant* there was 'dancing, piping, gaming, wakes, ales, bearbaiting and picnics,' and it was only with the gradual growth of the Puritan movement that religious insistences ate up the holiday licence.

But the Puritans did not gain their way without a struggle. A good half-century before the matter of Puritanism was finally brought to a head by the Civil War (1649), culminating dramatically in the execution of Charles I, a continual bickering between Puritans and the champions of the established order had already been the rule; and one small issue in all this was the question of Sunday Observance. Even in those days the arguments were much the same; in 1618, for instance, James I, remonstrating against Puritan prohibition of recreation and exercise after Sunday Service, complained that it –

*'*London,*' by Sir Walter Besant.*

'barreth the common and meaner sort of people from using such exercises as may make their bodies more able for war, when we or our successors shall have occasion to use them; and in place thereof sets up filthy tippling and drunkenness, and breeds a number of idle and discontented speeches in the ale-house; for when shall the common people have leave to exercise, if not upon Sundays and holidays, seeing they must apply their labour, and win their living, in all the working days.'

But the Puritans won. Even after the Restoration, in 1676, an Act of Parliament forbade Sunday trade, as well as all entertainments that must be paid for. In 1679 the Lord Mayor of London issued a Declaration penalising 'every profane curser and swearer,' drunkards and 'common haunters of ale-houses and taverns,' adding that –

'All persons using any unlawful exercise on the Lord's Day, or tippling in taverns, inns or ale-houses during divine service on that day, are to forfeit three shillings and four pence for every offence ... or ... to sit three hours in the stocks ... and no person may sit in the streets with herbs, fruits, or other things, to expose them for sale, nor no coachman may stand or ply in the streets on that day ...'

Only very recently did it cease to be *technically* proper to place people in the stocks for breaking the Sabbath, and very many Sunday observance laws still have a blind eye turned upon them, by police and public alike. It was in just this manner that the century following the Restoration unofficially lifted some of the weight off Sundays, although the process of relief was a very slow and gradual one. According to Trevelyan* the impression left by the Puritans never quite wore off:

'It is, indeed, remarkable how much of Puritan, or at least of strongly Protestant thought and practice, survived the political and ecclesiastical fall of the Puritan sect. Family prayer and Bible reading had become the national custom among the great majority of religious laymen, whether they were Churchmen or Dissenters. The English character had received an impression from Puritanism which it bore for the next two centuries, though it had rejected Puritan co-

---

**G. M. Trevelyan, 'History of England.'*

ercion. Even at the Restoration, when the very name of Puritan was a hissing and a reproach, when the gaols were crowded with harmless Quakers and Baptists, the Puritan idea of Sunday, as a day strictly set aside for rest and religious meditation, continued to hold the allegiance of the English people ...'

Even so, the eighteenth century did regain at least part of Sunday's former holiday atmosphere. But the relative freedom from restriction was not allowed to last for long. The rise of Evangelical Christianity, gaining strength at the beginning of the nineteenth century, brought with it the Sunday of Victorian days – intensified and extended church-going, family prayers, and rigid restriction of Sunday activities, even within the home, to the most sober and religious of sources.

To the Victorians, Sunday was a day to be devoted exclusively to church-going and religious contemplation. Here is a family where that ideal was faithfully carried out:

> 'We came down to breakfast at the usual time. My father prayed briefly before we began the meal; after it, the bell was rung, and, before the breakfast was cleared away, we had a lengthy service of exposition and prayer with the servants. If the weather was fine we then walked about the garden, doing nothing, for about half-an-hour. We then sat, each in a separate room, with our Bibles open and some commentary on the text beside us, and prepared our minds for the morning service. A little before 11 a.m. we sallied forth, carrying our Bibles and hymn books, and went through the morning service of two hours at the Room; this was the central event of Sunday.
>
> 'We then came back to dinner – curiously enough to a hot dinner, always with a joint, vegetables and puddings, so that the cook at least must have been busily at work – and after it my father and my stepmother took a nap – each in a different room, while I slipped out into the garden for a little while, but never venturing further afield. In the middle of the afternoon, my stepmother and I proceeded up the village to Sunday School, where I was early promoted to the tuition of a few very little boys. We returned in time for tea, immediately after which we all marched forth, again armed, as in the morning, with Bibles and hymn books, and we went

through the evening service, at which my father preached. The hour was already past my week-day bedtime, but we had another service to attend, the Believers' Prayer Meeting, which commonly occupied forty minutes more. Then we used to creep home, I often so tired that the weariness was like physical pain, and I was permitted, without further "worship", to slip upstairs to bed.'*

This is Sunday in an exceptionally religious household, but amongst the middle classes generally Sunday observance was not so very much less severe. Here, for instance, are the recollections of an elderly woman member of Mass-Observation's National Panel, of Sundays spent in her late Victorian childhood:

'In my early youth – my feelings about Sunday were suppressed rage at what I felt were illogical and absurd restrictions of our activities at home. I was forbidden to do my French homework then (which I loved and could do easily), but allowed to do "Scripture," which consisted of dry maps of the travels of the Apostles, etc., in whom I had no interest. Needlework was a crime, and yet I could "wash up" extra dishes after meals to get the maid off for her short time off duty. Tennis was an abominable sin, but walking was quite permissible. I could bang horribly at hymns on the piano, but not play anything pleasant. Church meant vile "best clothes" – tight hat, ditto collar, couldn't even pick flowers for fear they soiled my best gloves. When free of the Early Victorian father, I found Sunday a delightful day, on which to go out in the country taking food for the day, or to get jobs done which couldn't be fitted in on the other days.'

'When free of the Early Victorian father,' Sunday went fairly rapidly downhill. Towards the end of the century, for instance, the National Sunday League became active – organising facilities such as Sunday railway excursions at cheap rates, and in 1896 gaining the Sunday opening of museums and art-galleries. By the beginning of the new century, Sunday observance was relaxing a little. Even if the habits of the Sunday were still superficially preserved, attitudes were perhaps unwittingly beginning to lighten, and the Devil had his foot firmly in the door.

Here, for instance, is an account of the *Edwardian* Sunday,

**Edmund Gosse, 'Father and Son,' 1907.*

spent by the maidservant of a wealthy Church family; perhaps maidservants have always been inclined to frivolity – but to counter-balance that it must be remembered that this was a Bishop's household, presumably instructed in the proprieties of Sunday Observance:

> 'My mother was head housemaid in the family of a small-town Bishop. I always got the impression that Sunday was their best day of the week. Only essential work had to be done. Church twice a day, morning and evening; in Church the house staff were kept together, but the young men from the town would sit at the back of the Church and there would be some exchanging of smiles and glances; they would hover in the aisle as everyone went out and perhaps even find out your name and smuggle a note to you into the House to meet them in the Shrubbery. Officially speaking, courting was strictly forbidden by the mistress of the house, but no one took any notice of that, and Church was a very good way of getting to know young men other than the footmen and butlers. The only other way was the Sunday afternoon walk. That was the only time you were allowed out during the week and all the female staff went for a walk up Oxford Road in little groups, according to their job, supervised by their superiors. The young men from the town were there as well, of course, and again there would be glances and surreptitious smiles, and they might find out your name and send you a note. Sunday was a great day.'

Whether for better or worse the twentieth century, with its partial disintegration of religious belief and broadening of church outlook, has opened the door to brighter Sundays. A big step was taken in 1932 when Sunday cinemas became legal, together with Sunday (musical) concerts, and the Sunday opening of exhibitions, picture galleries, zoos, etc. Still forbidden are theatres, organised sports and Sunday trading, as well as circuses in many areas – and the Lord's Day Observance Society sees to it that they remain out of the question. Mr. Martin, Secretary of the Lord's Day Observance Society, told an investigator:

> 'In order to carry out our aims and objects we organise meetings – over a thousand were held last year – public demonstrations, services in churches and public halls, and Sunday

schools ... At the children's meetings the young people are asked to sign a pledge to observe the Sabbath day, and over 100,000 such pledges have been signed, quite voluntarily, in the past 15 years. As soon as the question of Sunday cinemas is broached, we rally our Defence Demonstrators at a meeting in the Town Hall and invite a prominent local person to preside. I firmly believe in carrying the fight to our opponents on all these issues.'

The battle goes on; lingering nineteenth century taboos leave Sunday a day of mild negatives, a nondescript day, neither one thing nor the other, no more a holiday than an opportunity for religious celebration.

CHAPTER VII
BRIGHT SPOTS

VICTORIAN SUNDAY was rigid, and present-day Sunday, except for the summer-time race to the country, seems merely quiet. But it would be wrong to give the impression that opportunities for brighter Sundays simply do not exist. Hammersmith, for instance, has its cinemas and Dance-Hall, even if little else in the way of large-scale Sunday facilities. And for Londoners, at least, there *are* entertainments, provided that they go out of their way to look for them. 'Petticoat Lane,' for instance, as described by one of our investigators:

> 'The London market known as Petticoat Lane covers the area of Middlesex Street and Wentworth Street and overflows into the many small side streets branching out from the two main roads. Looking down the "Lane" as far as the eye can see, stalls display every conceivable class of goods – shirts, handbags, cheap jewellery, dresses, gaudy statuettes, fruit and vegetables, jellied eels, barrels of herrings, salted and pickled, dress and costume materials, weight guesser – "Beat the Guesser to 4 lbs. Souvenir if he fails" – and a barrow piled high with wooden trays filled with doughnuts, with the young man in charge chanting monotonously ,"naw five a shilling, fresh doughnuts – five a shillin' fresh doughnuts." Passers-by walk mostly in pairs; the predominating age group is definitely under forty with a high percentage of young people in their late teens and mid-twenties. Almost entirely working-class people, neatly and quietly dressed, and there's quite a fair sprinkling of fur coats and hats and lined bootees.'

Where do the people come from, and what brings them to the Lane on the Sunday morning? Here is a young working woman to speak for herself:

> 'Well, I'm from Hayes. My friend and I have come down to Petticoat Lane to-day because she wants to buy a pair of

lined bootees and I wanted a pair of fur lined gloves. I've managed to get the gloves (shows investigator a pair of brown nappa-lined gloves, coney fur backed, for which she paid 35/-). Yes, I'm quite pleased with them and I'd quite a time bargaining with the old woman. That was the best part – I enjoyed that. I think that's what people come to Petticoat Lane for. It's fun. Now I was here before Christmas – you couldn't pass. It's not a good time now owing to the bus strike. People are frightened. Why do I come here? Well – there's nothing like it anywhere else in London. You'll find all sorts of people get to the Lane and it's the same instinct in them all – to try and get a bargain.'

Traders are mostly Jewish. Those holding the attention of the largest crowds are generally men in their early thirties, quite pleasant to look at, and with a non-stop flow of racy smutty talk, which keeps the crowd laughing uproariously. The selling technique is all the same – a racy and glib tongue, saucy insinuations. Here's Jackie J... selling dresses, attracting a huge crowd – men and women – while there are any number of dress stalls nearby with not a customer between them. Notice on stall reads: 'Jackie ... on the air again.' Jackie's selling dresses by the dozen:

'Be careful how you spend your money in Petticoat Lane. They say you're always caught. You've heard the old story they'll take your shirt off your back at one end of the Lane and by the time you get to the other end they've washed and pressed it and got it hung up on the staff for selling. But despite all the stories of getting done, look at the people that come here. You'll soon be seeing notices in the West End shops – Sales are on, and people'll be queueing up all night to get the bargain what's in the window, and when they get in the shop the assistant says (mimics) "Sorry, Moddom, but it's already sold." Serves you bloody well right. We have a bloody sale every time we open. Now here's a smart blouse – who'll give me a shilling for it. You will? Gawd blimey. Be careful how you spend your money. Now I'm going to take a dozen dresses, you can reserve any of them you like. Here's a lovely blue frock. WX made by Sally Slade of Regent Street, I'm not lying. The tab's on. See this green one – well it fell off the back of a van. It was *pushed off* – (loud laughter, women point to different dresses hanging on the rail). D'you

MEET YOURSELF ON SUNDAY

know I'll let you into a secret. At the last Command Performance I recognised thirty of my bloody dresses ... Now this one – this dress has been here for the last five years – I joined up because I couldn't bear to see it any longer, and I've been abroad for five years, and when I come back it was still here (laughter). Now here's a lovely jumper suit going half coupon rate. Now I'm not selling them at £4 apiece, but twenty-eight and six, and if those who want them will go inside they'll wrap them up for you (nearby shop)' ... Many women leave the crowd.

'Between twelve and one p.m. is the peak period. The noise is terrific. A disabled ex-service men's band plays 'When Irish Eyes are Smiling.' From a radio shop comes the tune and someone singing 'I belong to Glasgie.' Suitcase boys are getting frantic with their wares and shouting 'genuine Italian Nylons a dollar a pair.' The boy at the herring stall is still slicing up herrings. He's done nothing else all the morning but slice herrings and wrap them in greaseproof paper. Near a shoe stall a girl is trying on a pair of brown platform shoes with enormous heels. A barrow boy calls 'Sweet Almonds two shillings a quarter' and near him a man is selling puppies at 7/6d. a time. Lots of children gather round him saying 'Oh, isn't he sweet.' A baker's van adds to the confusion and people scramble out of the roadway ...

'1-30 to 2-0 p.m. Tradesmen dismantle their stalls. People leave the Lane for the open road. Policemen walk up and down the Lane, seeing all, hearing all but saying nothing. Prince Monolulu calls out 'I've got a hoss. I've got the tips for Wednesday's, Friday's and Saturday's races. Here is my office (producing paper) here is my card. My name is Rasputin Monolulu. The tip costs 2/– only.' Young man buys. Prince Monolulu 'shake hands for luck.' Young man shakes hands. The audience smile good-humouredly and wend their way ...'

Petticoat Lane is a bright spot of unusual character, an attraction that asks more of people than just to watch, and gives them correspondingly more in return. The people who go to Petticoat Lane have, to some extent, become part of the entertainment themselves; the principle is in many ways very similar in its spontaneity to that of the boisterous back-bantering Music

BRIGHT SPOTS

Hall of two generations ago. In Petticoat Lane there is little of the lethargy and aimlessness otherwise so common on Sundays.

There *are* other attractions on Sundays, but not many are so active or so animated as Petticoat Lane. The Hyde Park speakers for instance:

> Despite the cold weather there are some five or six well attended meetings. The Salvation Army has a platform with a crowd of about fifty people, largely working-class and predominantly men. Next door is the Communist Party platform, occupied by a tall intellectual-looking man in horn-rimmed glasses. He has the biggest crowd, about 400, almost entirely men, and again working-class. There are no interruptions, everyone seems interested. Next to him is a speaker with a down on Royalty – 'You lucky people, you can all go to work tomorrow, but I can't, I'm descended from Royalty.' Next speaker, with a large crowd of about 300, eighty per cent. men, is having a hard time from a sort of subdued heckling at the foot of the platform. Finally he invites the heckler up – who proceeds to be bitter and abusive about his predecessor, which the crowd don't like; shouts of 'You're a Fascist' – 'I'm not a Fascist' ... shouts of 'Sit down' ... A depressed looking middle-aged working man lights his cigarette and suddenly bawls at the speaker, quite irrelevantly, 'You didn't go over the top, mate, you didn't go over the top ...'

But Hyde Park 'Speakers' Corner' has, to some extent, deteriorated into a Sunday 'sight' at a different level not so very unlike the Tower of London or the Zoo. In any case, the speakers are by no means a new development. Beatrice Webb, 'mass-observing' in 1887, describes in her diary Sunday afternoon speakers in Victoria Park, East London:

> 'Sunday afternoon, a great time in Victoria Park, not confined to local people, but the meeting place of the enthusiasts and the odd-minded of the whole East End district. The first group we came to were congregating round a small organ; they were old men, women with children, and one or two strong youths; and they called themselves "The Elder Branch of Primitive Methodists" ... Some ten yards further, a small knot of working men crowded round two disputants, an English mechanic and a Russian emigrant ... The main crowds were gathered on a grand space under the trees.

Here was a nauseous nigger mouthing primitive methodism; back to back with him, facing another crowd, there was a messenger from the Hall of Science ... but the thickest crowd surrounded the banner of the Social democrat ...'*

Following up other Sunday attractions, we talked to the experts of the London Transport Executive about the pattern of Sunday travel. One, in charge of South London Buses, said:

'Sunday's routine starts with a "hard core" of regular travellers about 7-0 in the morning – the golfers, the fishers, and the first people going to the markets – these are the same type of people as used to go thirty years ago. Then there is a lull until ten, when the hikers and day-trippers go off, and at eleven o'clock the church-goers. At mid-day there is the pub travel and the first cemetery visitors. There is a lull through lunch time and then more movement in the afternoon to hospitals and cemeteries. A peak comes after tea when people are going *out* to cinemas and pubs, and *back* from museums and hospitals. From 7-0 to 8-30 there is a lull and then everybody starts coming back in a rush. In the summer, of course, there is a great extra traffic rush to the country, and to places like Richmond and Hampton Court; you get this in winter as well, so long as the weather is fine, but of course, much more in summer time ... '

Hospitals, museums, pubs, cinemas, cemeteries – not a very stimulating picture. In the summer, of course, there is the Zoo as well as the rush to the country to brighten things up. Even in winter-time there is still, as the bus experts say, a certain amount of park-strolling. In Kensington Gardens, for instance on a December Sunday afternoon:

'All about the Round Pond it is very crowded. Twelve sailing boats on the pond, and many children with their parents. (Yesterday there were nearly as many sailing boats, but children were often with nurses, not parents) ...'

And by the Serpentine a surreptitious game of football behind the policeman's back:

'Three groups of three, four and five boys, kicking footballs around near the Serpentine. When only one group was

*Beatrice Webb, 'My Apprenticeship'.

BRIGHT SPOTS

playing a policeman came up and told them to stop. Twenty minutes later, when the policeman was out of sight, all three groups were playing again ...'

Even the brightest spots on a winter's Sunday are sometimes rather tarnished. And as the sun goes down the festival atmosphere becomes still harder to discover. Even the Sunday supper at a cafe is a mild affair, as these observations made at one of the London Corner Houses show:

> 'At 8-40 p.m. – Brasserie full, but not crowded; very easy to find an empty table even though about a quarter of the room is roped off behind "No service" placards. The orchestra is in full swing, playing very light music. The noise of chatter is subdued, even in pauses, whilst the orchestra rests. People are chiefly in couples, but sometimes of the same sex, and sometimes alone. Fairly equally young and middle-aged, and mostly lower middle or skilled working class. Most are eating hot suppers or high teas, and talking very quietly ... Neatly dressed, for the most part, in Sunday clothes ... At about 9 o'clock some of the lights are turned down, the orchestra packs up, the waitresses hurry things up by distributing checks. By 9-30 practically everyone is gone ...'

But that is Sunday in winter. The heat of the summer sun endows lounging with added purpose and pleasure, and opens the door to Sunday spent out of town, in the open air.

CHAPTER VIII
SUNDAY EXCURSION

THERE IS no doubt that the 'brightest' spots on Sunday belong to summer rather than winter. A summer's day in the country or at the seaside has an air of luxury and exuberance which can tempt thousands out of town. On a July Sunday during the long 1949 heatwave, for instance, *one Londoner in every* 287 took a day-return ticket to Southend alone; here is an account of what may have happened when they got there: a day at a South-coast seaside resort, one hot Sunday in July:

'It is a hot summer's day and holiday-makers in their hundreds flock to the sea-front. The time is 10-30 a.m., but even at this early hour deck chairs running the length of the promenade are nearly all taken. The beach, too, is crowded, with two-thirds of the people sitting on deck chairs and the remaining third—mostly teen-agers – sunbathing on the pebbly beach. The majority are reading their Sunday newspapers, but the general atmosphere is much too distracting, and reading isn't really taken seriously. It doesn't take long before newspapers fall on people's laps while they look around, content to drink in the general holiday scene: women in their gaily coloured summer frocks; children paddling in the water; half-a-dozen lads – 12-14 years of age – carrying a tangerine-coloured rubber dinghy to the water's edge; a motor-speedboat swishing by leaving a trail of white foam; swimmers bobbing up and down in the water. Then a dog jumps in the water to retrieve a ball, and, coming out, shakes himself free of water, and at the same time wets everyone near him, much to the delight of adults and children alike.

'Time 11-0 – 12-0. There are many more families on the beach. A middle-aged man, heavily built, very hairy chested, waddles down to the sea. Overheard from young couple:
27 year old wife: 'He's got some flesh round his middle. I reckon he's got a nerve to want to show off a figure like that.'
30 year old husband: 'And I bet he's a good swimmer – those fat people generally are powerful swimmers.'

SUNDAY EXCURSION

'It's not without interest that we watch him take to the water. Sure enough he proves to be a very powerful swimmer.

'Young boy, about 17 years of age, in a very vivid canary-yellow sports-shirt plays the concertina, while three of his pals, same age, potential spiv types, join in the singing. Children and young girls crowd round – they too join in. And the feelings of holiday-makers are pretty mixed:

33 *year old woman:* 'Oh, that's a bit livelier – they *could* do with a bit of a band here to cheer things up.'

50 *year old man:* 'Dreadful ! It shouldn't be allowed on the beach on a Sunday.'

'Two pretty young flappers about 16 years of age sit on the beach near two sailors. Sailors ogle flappers; flappers not above ogling sailors; flappers do a lot of giggling. Twenty-five minutes pass – flappers start a strip-tease act ... sailors very interested and watch the process of disrobing stage by stage. Off comes frock, petticoat, knickers, until both reveal the briefest of brief one-piece bathing suits.

Flapper to sailors: 'Aren't you going in for a dip, or are you afraid of the water ?'

Sailor (smiling): 'Well, it's a bit of a novelty for us – but we'll chance it.'

'Girls cover heads with white bathing caps and gingerly walk on the pebbly beach. Very soon they're in the water; both good swimmers. Ten minutes later: sailors start undressing, and in no time they're in the water playfully splashing the girls with water and making themselves a nuisance generally.

'Time 12 – 1 p.m. Beach scene: mothers and fathers dozing or semi-dozing in deck chairs, while young people splash about in the water or relax or sunbathe on the beach; young girls and sailors sprawled out flat on the beach; young spivs still crooning sentimental songs to the accompaniment of the concertina; hundreds of cars lined up alongside curb near pier and stretching as far as one can see. A dozen or so young girls and boys – day trippers – wearing paper hats with huge feathers; children and adults drinking fizzy bottles of lemonade or eating ice-cream; dogs barking, children laughing, while at every turn one sees sailors from English, Indian, American and Norwegian ships and hears the babbling of their different accents and languages. And meantime there's a steady exodus from the beach as holiday-makers drift off for their mid-day meal.

'Time 2-20 p.m. At the Punch and Judy, thirty to forty kiddies are sitting in the enclosure with as many adults standing in the rear. Punch is holding a string of sausages and rejoicing in the fact that there's going to be 'sausages for tea – sausages for tea – now I'll go and get the frying pan.' But during his absence the crocodile appears and wants to eat Punch's sausages. This sends the kiddies into a frenzy as they scream, 'It's the crocodile.' Punch takes hold of his mallet and wants to beat the crocodile but he suddenly disappears:

Punch: Where is he?

Kiddies (hysterically): There he is.

Punch: Where?

Again the kiddies yell – 'There he is behind you!'

But the crocodile is as elusive as ever. Nemesis overtakes him and eventually Punch tracks him down and hangs him, much to the delight of the kiddies, and the adults too. Man comes round with collecting box. Most kiddies put a copper or so in it. With the show over the kiddies don't budge, but stick tight to their seats for the next showing. The investigator asks

SUNDAY EXCURSION

little boy about seven years if he liked the show, and what he liked best. His name is Tommy:
Tommy: I liked Judy's ghost best, because she chases him around, but he hangs her up on a stick and throws her downstairs – that's very funny.'

'Time 4 p.m. At the Pier head an orchestra is playing light popular music of the *Tea for Two* – *Student Prince* variety, to a large audience of 400-500 people, mostly working class and middle-aged. High percentage of the men reading their Sunday newspapers and the women knitting. About a dozen people leaning over the Pier railing watching men fishing from boats. Looking into the water one can easily see the fish jumping about on the water's surface. A middle-aged woman joins her husband:

'I've just had my fortune told, it says I'm going to meet a tall, dark and handsome husband (playfully puts hand on husband's cheek) and you're *not* tall, and *not* dark, and you're *not* handsome. I suppose they're all the same, and that if you go on the machine long enough you'd get the same ones in the end. Still I suppose it's worth a penny for the laugh you get out of it.'

It's worth more than a penny to spend Sunday at the seaside, but it costs more than a penny too, and not everyone can afford it. But for youth, at least, there are ways of getting out into the country more or less for nothing. Membership of the London region of the Youth Hostel Association, for instance, has more than doubled itself since before the war – and an important part of their work is the organisation of week-end cycling and walking clubs.

Their expressed aim is to encourage 'care and love of the country-side'; but there are plenty of other cycling clubs whose purpose is, quite simply, to go cycling. Any of them can be seen, speeding out of town, almost any Sunday – swarms of cyclists in a stream of mainroad traffic. Here is an account of Sunday with a Y.H.A. cyclist club:

'Thursday is club night for the local group of the Y.H.A., and one of the main purposes of the evening is to get names and arrange outings for the Sunday walks and cycle runs. On the Sunday, walkers and cyclists meet at about 10 a.m., usually at a local station. There are anything from six to twenty cyclists, young men and women, ages ranging from 16 to 24 or so – all in shorts unless it is particularly cold when one or two may wear plus fours. The girls have a friendly rivalry to see who can wear the gayest and most unusual beret – for instance, with the longest pom-pom attachment; the men wear, if anything, a black beret with Y.H.A. badge.

'At about 10-15 to 10-30, after the 'same' latecomers have arrived with the 'same' excuses, the leader suggests starting. This is usually a long drawn out affair. Machines are often in a bad state of repair and need repeated adjustments. There is a lot of back chat and friendly abuse. Sheila, a 21 year old typist in a city office (friend of all in the group, always to be relied on to raise a laugh) is still re-packing her kit or eating a sandwich, shouting 'wait for me.' But after a last minute checking tyre pressures, there is a straggling start, and within about a mile from the starting point the group forms itself into two abreast, as chance or choice dictates. Sheila's 18 year old brother Stan, an apprentice mechanic, is usually to the fore of the formation, Sheila to the rear. If Betty, 22 year old film continuity girl, is also out, she and Sheila are together throughout the day, sometimes at the rear of a close formation, sometimes half a mile behind the rest. Conversation is either irresponsible banter, frivolous, mildly flirtatious or else technical – about cycle speeds, cycle difficulties, cycle preferences, etc. Sometimes, after a friendly dispute about speeds, the men take the opportunity to 'bash' – that is to cycle all out and indulge in time trials; when this happens the group splits into two, and the less energetic spend their Sunday at a slower pace.

'The leader usually has a particular pub in mind for the midday stop which sets the limit to the day's run. Everybody has sandwiches which they eat together inside the pub or out, with beer for the men and shandy or soft drinks for the girls. Lunch lasts till closing time – sometimes an hour or sometimes longer ...

'Time of arriving home depends largely on the time of year, averaging round about 7-0 or 8-0 p.m. After a hard day every one is glad to get home early, but if the pace has been leisurely, the last part of the return may be even more so, stopping at a fair-ground, a pub or a cafe in the nearby towns. Sometimes a particular clique of eight or nine might finish up

SUNDAY EXCURSION

at the cinema, or at one of the members' homes (usually if the parents are out), when an impromptu party would result, with the emphasis on flirting, mild necking and generally enjoying themselves.'

That is Sunday in summer – Sunday at its noisiest, most crowded, and, for some at least, at its most fulfilled.

CHAPTER IX

SUNDAY JAIL

ALL SUNDAYS cannot be spent out of doors, and generally speaking it is difficult to avoid the conclusion that Sunday – in winter particularly – is normally quiet, perhaps dull. For most people there is plenty of time, but little to do. The same pattern appears almost everywhere; in its bleakest form it is even apparent in prison.

An ex-prisoner, Mass-Observation trained in objective reporting, wrote us the following account of Sunday in Jail:

'Preparations for Sunday commence on the Saturday evening. Whilst prisoners are locked in their cells sewing mailbags, a warder brings round to each cell in turn, boot polish and brush; with this each prisoner has to clean his boots and shoes – boots are worn on each weekday, and the shoes are only worn on a Sunday. Saturday evening is the only time that one cleans boots and shoes. Also being taken around to each cell is a shaving brush, soap and safety razor, which each prisoner uses in turn. One sometimes has the opportunity to shave during the week, but one always has a shave on the Friday or Saturday, in readiness for "Sunday."

'First thing Sunday morning is "Slops out," a little later than any other day. On a Sunday prisoners wear Sunday Clothes – special clothes which one must *only* wear on a Sunday. "Special" only in as much as they are not worn so often as weekday clothes – they are the same drab colour and the same badly cut and ill-fitting garments as the others.

'After breakfast (the meal does not vary on a Sunday – mug of tea, plate of porridge, cob and pat of margarine) each prisoner is given a "tie." These ties are only issued on a Sunday morning and are collected every Sunday evening.

'Instead of mail-bag sewing or digging, or whatever "party" or "shop" one may be in during the week, Sunday provides a rest from this. Mid-morning all prisoners (except those whose religion will not allow them) are marched out of

MEET YOURSELF ON SUNDAY

the cell into the yard. From there they are marched to the prison church. They march up the aisle in single file, and seats are filled from left to right, starting at the front. There are very few prisoners who do not avail themselves of the opportunity of Sunday church. This complete change from prison cell solitude, this listening to Bach and Handel on the organ, and the opportunity to yell loudly during hymn singing, provides a "release" and freedom which has to be experienced to be fully comprehended. The service is orthodox Church of England, with a Church of England minister officiating.

'After church, if the weather is reasonably fine, all prisoners march round and round the "ring" – the prison yard – a longer period of exercise on Sunday morning and afternoon than during the week. Either in the yard or in the cell block the Deputy Governor reads out the previous day's football and sports results for the information of prisoners. He will also give a brief summary of the news, as printed in the *Sunday Times.* Prisoners then return to their cells and await dinner – the same insipid and insufficient meal that may be had on a week-day.

'Mid-afternoon, another church service, same procedure as before; after which more exercising, walking round and round the prison yard, and then back to the cells, a wait and tea – cob, marge, cocoa and a small piece of cheese – the cheese being part of the Sunday ritual. After tea nothing, just the locked door and one's own thoughts.'

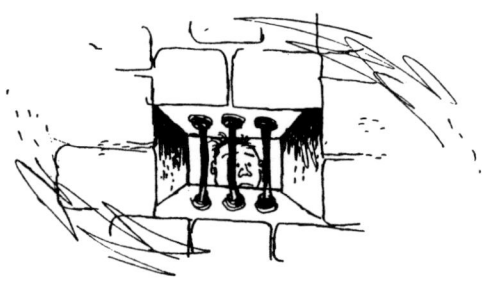

CHAPTER X

THOUGHTS BEHIND LOCKED DOORS

PRISON SUNDAY comes to an early end with 'locked doors and one's own thoughts.' Even out of jail, limited Sunday facilities put a metaphorical lock to the doors behind which families play cards, listen to the wireless, do odd jobs, and – except on the finer days of summer – indulge in 'nothing in particular.' How do people feel about this more or less forcible confinement one day out of seven? Is it a question of reluctant leisure?

Putting the question, in various forms, to the 'man in the street'* we found that although most people welcome Sundays on the whole, considerably fewer are entirely satisfied with them. For instance, two-thirds of all those we questioned said they liked Sundays – yet every second person also suggested ways in which they could be made more enjoyable, particularly brightened up. Sunday contentment may be a matter of making the best of a bad job.

Reasons for liking Sundays are usually more or less negative; people enjoy Sunday chiefly because they do not have to work, but also because it provides a release from week-day routine. A middle-aged housewife, for instance, glad of the chance to relax, is quite willing to accept and enjoy Sunday as a day of rest:

> 'I think I like Sunday, because it's a rest from every other day. I appreciate it because I can spend the day quietly, seeing relatives. After all, I live in one mad rush all the week. I've an afternoon job as well, and it's one long rush, getting

---

About one hundred people were interviewed, equal numbers men and women, over and under forty, and so proportioned from the point of view of social class as to be more or less representative of the population at large. All the interviewing took place in Hammersmith. Although this Borough offers its residents rather more opportunities for Sunday entertainment, contentment there is unlikely to be much, if at all, more pronounced than it is anywhere else (at least in London) – since even in Hammersmith large scale amusement facilities do not extend far beyond the customary cinemas and pubs.

everything ready and being on time. I don't really get much time to myself other than Sunday.'

Draughtsman's Wife, 50.

But for others rest may come to include at least a little restlessness; then the emphasis moves on to *difference*, rather than *relaxation*. This elderly housewife, for instance, groping amongst the right and wrongs of Sunday observance, is on her way to wanting something more than the opportunity to rest:

> 'Sunday *was* supposed to be a day of rest, but it depends on what people mean by a "day of rest." Does it mean sitting in a chair? I sometimes think it's a day away from things in general, away from what you do in the week.'
>
> Building worker's wife, 62.

For people thinking along these lines, Sunday needs to be as different as possible from the rest of the week. Some are content to make it different for themselves; others feel that the more entertainment they are offered, the better. A middle-aged plumber, for instance, who feels that church is 'too depressing':

> 'I regard Sunday as a holiday – let me put it this way. I don't think of Sundays as a sacred day, but as a day of rest from work – a change to ordinary everyday life. I enjoy my work immensely, but speaking broadly I look upon Sundays as a day of rest from the workaday week. And as such I think that facilities for sport should be available to those that want it – it shouldn't only be allowed but encouraged, and places of entertainment should be open, particularly as churchgoing only appeals to a very small percentage of the people. Put in a nutshell my idea of Sundays is it's a break from the humdrum ordinary work of the week. It represents the one day's break in the week when you can meet your friends, visit relatives, or catch up with your correspondence – not a day of religion – church doesn't interest the present generation – that's of the past simply because it's too depressing, the vicar talks in monotone all the time; as for the traditional "Monday Blues," in my opinion it doesn't exist – it's more likely to be round about Wednesday or Thursday, not Monday, because people have been out in the open on Sundays and feel all the better for it.'

How many people have the chance on Sundays of getting a 'change to ordinary everyday life'? To some, especially men, it is a change to be at home with their family, in a position to indulge in all the relaxations denied them during the week. Being able to do as they please, having the opportunity for odd jobs about the house, visiting friends and relatives, getting up late, having all their family around them, sinking into a pleasant relaxed atmosphere – all these are mentioned by smallish numbers as reasons for enjoying Sunday; moreover, except for the housewife, all of them involve a change from the week-day routine. But these things tend to be enjoyed largely by those people who are fairly contentedly steeped in the family atmosphere, and to whom Sunday gives sufficient leisure to enjoy it. Young men and women, restless as well as less reconciled to home life, inclined to seek their 'change' away from its domestic limitations, tend to be most bored by Sundays:

> 'I don't like Sundays much. It's all right for the rest, but there's not much to do. Monday? I rather like it – I hate to be at home.'
>
> Woman shop assistant, 19.

> 'Sunday is a dreary day. Everywhere is dead. The children aren't allowed to play in the street. It's "clear away from here," wherever they go. Father wants to sleep in the afternoon, why I don't know. But it's the only day a man doesn't go to work, and where is there for him to go but the pub, and you can't afford that. There ought to be more entertainment for children, not just to get them out of the way, but so that they like to go out; my little boy doesn't go to Sunday school, it's so dreary – he wanted to go, but came home and said, "They're so miserable – you all have to sit there and you mustn't make a noise." If only they told little stories and made it interesting ...'
>
> Metal worker's wife, 34.

And housewives – particularly working-class housewives – are inclined to resent the extra work that Sunday involves:

> 'It's the hardest day of the week; everybody's up late, and you're behind with the tidying up. Then I've got to round up the children and get them ready for Sunday school. I simply can't bear Sundays; it's a day which everyone regards as a rest day except for me. They all go out; my man sleeps in a chair; and I'm left with a load of dishes to wash up. I

MEET YOURSELF ON SUNDAY

hate Sundays. I dread to see it coming. It's the one day you're supposed to rest, and yet with a family how can a *woman* rest.'
Taxidriver's wife, 40.

We asked two groups of schoolgirls to write an account of how they feel about Sundays, and how they spend them. The youngest group, a class of twelve and thirteen-year-olds in an East End secondary school, for the most part enjoyed Sunday very much; but usually their contentment derived from Sunday's quietness and peacefulness, its value as a day they could spend at home with their families. For these younger, pre-adolescent children, Sunday is seldom dull:

'I got up at 7 o'clock – washed and did my hair. I thought I looked reasonably tidy, but my cousins who were staying with me (aged 18 and 21 – girls) evidently thought different. They told me I nearly scraped my hair out and did it again for me. My parents were away for the week-end, so I was with my cousins. I had an egg for breakfast, and my cousin spilt some coffee over my blue dress. At 10-30 I started out for church. I got there at 11 o'clock – the service was boring – about cutting heads off or something.

'At 12-15 I came out from church and went home. It was cooking the dinner that sticks in my memory. We put the potatoes on but they smoked horribly. When we had burned through the saucepan, we thought maybe it would be better with water in it. It was, but then my cousin Mary arrived. Thank goodness she can cook. (By that time I was foreseeing sandwiches for dinner). Mary cooked the rest of the dinner, and, although it tasted a bit queer, it was eatable. The cousins who were with me were Mary and Molly, twins aged 18, Doris aged 21, and later Len her husband (I don't know his age). In the afternoon Len arrived and I took the dogs for a walk, as I don't like Len. I saw Mr. Todd's boy – he must be about 23. He stuck his tongue out at me, so I stuck mine out at him. Unfortunately an acquaintance of my mother's got between us and she thought I was poking my tongue at her. I met two of my friends and went with them until 5 o'clock. I then went home for my tea, we had cream slice. In the evening we had the wireless on and Molly was teaching me to dance. We made a lot of noise, but we enjoyed ourselves.

MEET YOURSELF ON SUNDAY

'At 8 o'clock I went to see my friend and I stayed at her house until 10 o'clock, when I came home to bed.'

'I like Sundays because they are different. Also on Sunday people take their time and don't rush about. I go to Church and enjoy myself. We have a nice dinner on Sunday. I can wear what I like. I like going to church because we have to kneel down and the board that I kneel on squeaks as it is broken. Also there is a rather dignified old gentleman dressed in a long black gown – every time they say "Holy, Holy, Holy" he bends down to the altar. I am looking at the back view, and all I can see is a rather large seat coming up and suddenly a very small head appearing. This amuses us, although other people can never see what we are laughing at.'

Schoolgirls, 13 years, 3 months.

In childhood, incidents acquire the importance of events, and there is an element of adventure about the trivialities of the home. Usually the family plays an outstanding part in enjoyment of Sunday, it is largely for the sake of home and parents that childhood Sundays are pleasurable:

'I do like Sundays, because it is quite quiet and peaceful, and all my family is at home.'

12 years, 11 months.

'I like Sundays because I wake my mother with a cup of tea. I like church. I like taking the puppy for a walk. I like Sunday's dinner, and Sunday's breakfast.'

13 years, 3 months.

'I do like Sundays, because it is so quiet and peaceful, and I like the sound of Church bells.'

12 years, 7 months.

'I like Sundays because my father is at home, and we always have something nice to eat for tea, and we don't have to go on errands like Saturday, and you have more spare time, and I like going to Sunday school.'

12 years, 5 months.

But adolescence brings with it broadened horizons, restlessness, a vague desire for something more than the immediate family. Sundays are enjoyed less, unless they provide something of the desired opportunities for more sophisticated activity. This becomes clear in analysis of Sunday essays of older children – this time a group of fifteen and sixteen-year-old West London schoolgirls. Here for instance, is an adolescent Sunday, mildly enjoyed, vaguely unsatisfying:

'I got up at 9-30 a.m. and went down to breakfast in my dressing gown. When I had finished, I dressed myself, and then, at my little brother's request, I helped him to clear out his toys, in view of Christmas being near at hand. After this somewhat lengthy procedure, I went with him for a walk, he being on his bike. When we returned we had our usual well-cooked Sunday dinner, and after my mother had put my brother to bed, I helped her to wash the dishes. I ought to explain that my father is away at the moment. In the afternoon I duly departed to Crusaders, which is a type of Bible-class. I always enjoy myself here, especially this Sunday, as there was a Christmas feeling in the air. On my arrival at home, my little brother greeted me eagerly, and showed me the picture he had got from Sunday School. Then we listened to Community Hymn Singing, and afterwards we had tea. Then we settled down in front of the fire and talked with continuous interruptions from my brother.

At 7-30 p.m. he promptly went to bed, and my mother and I settled down to a pleasant evening. Somehow we got talking of the past, and the time just slipped by, and when we next looked up at the clock it was 10-30 p.m. So, I quickly went to bed as I had school in front of me to-morrow. I treat this Sunday as a typical one in my life – *nothing particular ever happens, and yet I would not call it dull.*

The only thing that would make a difference to my Sunday, is the return of my father, and that, fortunately, will have happened before the next Sunday comes round.'

15 years, 5 months.

Much more *positively* enjoyed, at this age, is the Sunday which provides continuous activity and companionship *outside the home:*

'I awoke at about 9-30 a.m., and a few minutes later my mother greeted me with a cup of tea and a biscuit. I scanned the pages of the *Sunday Pictorial*, and noticed an article about Princess Margaret on the rather late nights she has been having lately. I hurriedly dressed in my tennis togs – gulped down another cup of tea, munched a piece of toast, and dashed out of the house, already ten minutes late for my tennis date. As it happened I was earlier than my friend, and we enjoyed a short, but sweet, game.

'I arranged to meet her at 2-15 (knowing it would be 2-45 before she turned up) to go ice-skating at Richmond. I cycled home and, as usual, starving hungry, I had a second breakfast. After this I peeled the apples and made the pastry for the apple tart for dinner, and escaped to another friend's house a little way down the road. There we discussed the previous night's dance, and which boys had interested us. The time flew, and rushing home I tore upstairs to dress myself for skating. My mother fussed round me and nagged me about my unpolished boots, my untidy hair and other seemingly trivial things. I had a little lunch although I was not very hungry, and, as usual, was late for my appointment. As we were both late our bus seemed to crawl to Richmond. In the dressing room a loud hubbub of girlish giggles and laughs greeted us. On the ice we were greeted with one or two whistles, which modestly we ignored. Several boys took it into their heads to throw ice at us, which appeared to be their idea of getting acquainted ...'

15 years, 9 months.

Quite clearly it is impossible to say categorically whether people like Sunday or not. Contentment depends on age, sex and background, as much as on the opportunities available and individual differences of personality. But on the whole the family Sunday is satisfying chiefly to those for whom the family holds the attraction of restful enjoyment, that is, the family-engrossed man at work all the week, and children. For younger people and adolescents, on the other hand, Sunday can easily seem unsatisfying and restrictive, and for the housewife it may be a long day of continuous labour. Perhaps the best way of summing up the hypothetical *average* Sunday, would be to say, in the cautious words of the schoolgirl quoted on the preceding page – 'nothing particular ever happens, and yet I would not call it dull.'

CHAPTER XI

SABBATH SURVIVALS

SUNDAY EMERGES as a day of negative opportunities for the most part mildly enjoyed ('I would not call it dull'). Possibly the only way to transform it into a day of more positive individuality would be either to grant it full holiday opportunities, or else to revive its religious values and associations. Is this second alternative a practicable one? How far do present-day trends encourage it?

The Gallup Poll Sunday figures quoted earlier showed that roughly 15 people out of every 100 go to church every Sunday, and a 1946 Mass-Observation survey of religious beliefs showed that in Hammersmith –

> One person in four openly doubts the existence of a Deity – one in twenty expressing definitely atheistic views. There are exactly twice as many non-believers among the younger generation as among the old – 36 per cent. of the under-forties and 18 per cent. of the over forties.*

Religious belief is least frequent amongst members of the younger generation; and even amongst those who still retain their religion, belief is very often vague and ill-defined, with little or no impact on daily life and behaviour:

> Of those who say they believe in a Deity one in five are definite in their assertion that they do not believe in a life after death; one-half say they never go to church, or only go for weddings, funerals and such-like. A quarter never pray, or pray only in church.*

In our present survey very few explicitly gave religious reasons for liking Sunday, and most of these were elderly. The Sunday attitude of this 83-year-old widow, for instance, is exceptional:

*'*Puzzled People*', by Mass-Observation, published by Gollancz, 1947. Similar results emerged from a 1947 Mass-Observation Survey made on a larger scale all over the country.*

MEET YOURSELF ON SUNDAY

'On Sunday I just do ordinary housework, that has to be done. Then I get out my Bible and have my own Service. I don't go in for all these humbug amusements on Sunday, it should be kept for the Lord, within reason ... God made Sunday for a day of rest, and we upset it with all these pictures and that.'

Widow, old age pensioner, 83.

And a Christian Scientist:

'I like Sundays, because we're Christian Scientists. We look forward to Sunday and Wednesday evenings, because we get such an awful lot of help from the Christian Science Services.'

Single woman, 60, middle-class.

These are unusually enthusiastic church-goers. But there is something of the same feeling amongst one who only visits church occasionally – a furniture salesman, middle-aged, for whom Sunday is unquestionably a *religious* day of rest:

'I definitely look forward to Sundays – it's a day to be spent quietly and peacefully, and when one can forget business. It's nice to go to Church occasionally – personally I always feel better for it. I like to take it easy and try to keep it different – to feel I'm not tied to do anything, that I can choose to spend the day in the sort of way I like. I like to feel it *is* a day of rest.'

But such signs of even vaguely religious associations with Sunday are comparatively rare. They might, of course, in any case remain mostly unspoken, but symptoms of underlying attitudes generally come to the surface somewhere. Possibly there is something of this in the reply of the 25-year-old bank-clerk, for instance, who enjoys Sunday, amongst other reasons, because –

'... the home atmosphere generally is better on Sundays, I put it down that they've all been to church.'

Even amongst the irreligious, then, enjoyment of Sunday's rest and leisure may derive from some at least *half-aware* religious satisfaction. But at a more conscious level it is doubtful whether many people even hazily attribute any kind of religious value to Sundays, nowadays. And much of the drift from realising Sunday as the 'Lord's Day', to asking of it only non-religious relaxation,

SABBATH SURVIVALS

has occurred during a single lifetime. A middle-aged man, for instance, who describes himself as an atheist ('I think religion would be lovely if it were true') and likes Sunday as a day of relaxation ('I work hard all the week and am only too glad to get out and hit a little ball') had purely religious associations for Sunday in his youth:

> 'As a child I was deeply religious. My people brought me up to go to church, and I was a choirboy, and went to the Band of Hope, the league of this and that. I really thought there was a God in heaven. I used to enjoy Sunday, because I believed in God.'
>
> Managing Director, 63.

Sunday is slowly losing at least the outward trappings of its former religious meaning, even though it still retains many of the older Sabbath restrictions. And although it is outside our scope to make predictions on this point, there seems nothing at present to suggest any likelihood of a wide-scale revival of popular religious interest, a development which alone would render feasible any real return to the Sunday of positive religious values and enjoyment. Sunday, as the 'Lord's Day', is slowly disintegrating; is there a corresponding growth of the Sunday festival spirit?

CHAPTER XII

SUNDAY FANTASY

> 'Tis sweet to him who all the week
> Through city crowds must push his way,
> To stroll alone through field and woods
> And hallow thus the Sabbath day.'
>
> Coleridge: *Home-Sick.*

IT IS DIFFICULT to outline trends when the past is so much more difficult to penetrate than the present. But it is possible, roughly at least, to assess the extent to which people – particularly young people whose present inclinations may foreshadow the general attitudes of the future – dream of something different. Probing for day-dreams, we discovered that every second person says that he would like to spend Sundays as he does at present, and most of the remainder want a more interesting Sunday – usually away from their home town. A 35-year-old porter, for instance, vaguely discontented with his customary way of spending Sunday ('a drink mid-day, and a walk in the afternoon') says:

> 'I'd like to spend it out in the open air, if I could afford it – to go right out of London on that day.'

A young unemployed building worker, whose ideal was to spend Sunday with 'a nice trip to the country', is bored with Sundays as they are at present (a stroll, the pictures, then bed or the pub):

> 'There's nowhere to go and nothing to do. I just dread the day – there's no amusements, no pictures until four o'clock, and the pubs don't open until eleven – and then they're not open until the evening.'

And a 25 year-old clerk, who spends Sunday at home doing odd jobs, going for a walk, having a drink with his wife, would really like to be 'out in the country, sitting down and relaxing and thinking about other things'.

SUNDAY FANTASY

What does this urge to the country reflect? Making the best of the only available facilities? Desire for a change? Or romantic day-dreams of an idyllic countryside, most satisfying whilst they remain unrealised? It is true that during the summer thousands do pour out of the large towns, country-wards. But it is interesting that this dream of the countryside has cropped up in previous surveys, often unaccompanied by any serious attempt

to transform it into reality. In a 1947 Mass-Observation survey on gambling, for instance, we asked people what they would do if they made a really big win. Again and again the reply was to retire into a cottage in the country; some winners may in fact have taken such a step, but we have come across none of them ourselves. Similarly, a survey on holidays showed that far more people said they would like to go to a quiet seaside resort than actually went there; instead, in practice, they often went to Blackpool or some such place in no way corresponding to their dreams.

Economic and practical considerations, of course, play no small part in producing this gulf between dreams and reality. Certainly, as our interviews show, there would be more people going to the country on Sundays if all who wished could afford it; but is it also possible that fantasy does not always *intend* transformation into practice?

What else would people like to do on Sundays? Ideas for a brighter Sunday are usually very mild, sometimes startlingly so. A 56 year-old lorry-driver, for instance, who does nothing in particular on Sundays at present, unless it is 'helping the wife to clear up':

> 'I'd really like to go out in the evening – have a drink, or go to the pictures.'

A shorthand-typist, 25 years old:

> 'I'd like either to go away for the week-end – and stay with friends, or else go to a concert on Sunday afternoon.'

And a middle-aged working-class housewife, wistfully:

> 'I used to go out fishing. I like fishing, it rests the nerves, it steadies you.'

In fact, for the housewife, overwhelmed with extra work on Sundays, the ideal is nothing more riotous than a rest:

> 'Oh, if I had the chance I'd like a cold dinner, then there'd be no cooking and I could sit down and read in the afternoon – and I'd like to go to Church in the evening.'
>
> Housewife, 40.

It is clear enough that few people want a wildly exciting Sunday, but at the same time many would welcome more opportunities for non-religious pleasures. At the moment, however, large numbers of people are wary not only of asking for a brighter Sunday, but even of thinking the desire to themselves. The conflict between deep-seated moral sanctions and the newer desire to escape from the restrictions of negativity, is still very strong:

> 'I don't know really how I would like to spend Sunday. It's nice to have a nice quiet day – but I think I'd like to go out to some little amusement. It's nice to sit by the fire – but it's nice to go out. Mind you, I don't mind anyone calling, I mean I'd answer the door.'
>
> Working class housewife, 34.

At the moment at least there is unlikely to be any *clamour* for extended Sunday entertainment – although the ground is cleared of widespread opposition to it. For some years now, in

MEET YOURSELF ON SUNDAY

spite of the Lord's Day Observance Society's increasing membership, only a fairly small minority of the population has been against Sunday entertainment. War-time surveys on Sunday theatres, for instance, indicated that, in London at least, only about one person in nine is actually against the idea, although questioning on this subject produced an unusually high degree of uncertainty and prevarication. Similarly, a recent survey made nationally by Mass-Observation for the *Daily Graphic* on the subject of Sunday games showed that three people out of every five were in favour of playing games on Sundays: the North (particularly Scotland) was more opposed to the idea than the South (particularly London), and women rather more than men, but the most striking difference was between young and old; *three-quarters of all young people under twenty-four approve of Sunday games against only half the over forty-fives. It is to youth that the brighter Sunday is particularly important.*

Even in Sabbath-jealous Scotland there is a good deal of feeling that Sundays are unharmed by healthy amusement:

'Well, I fancy Sunday's just as good as any other day. I believe in God and the Bible, but I don't see why they shouldn't play after church is finished.'

Unemployed gravedigger, 52, Scotland.

'Oh well, I don't altogether condemn it. If the bowling greens were open on Sunday, I'd go and play. There's no harm in good clean games on Sunday, so long as you go to Church in the morning. We're too damn straight-laced in Scotland – there's no telling what people get up to behind their drawn blinds at night.'

Fishmonger, 50, Scotland.

And to Scotland, 'strait-laced' or not, belongs the final word on what people really want of Sundays. At the Glasgow opening of a new social club for young people, flying squads were called out to control a crowd of 10,000 youths and girls seeking admission.* Brighter Sundays could hardly be given a more flattering welcome.

*See 'Full Enjoyment', by Norman Crosby.

CHAPTER XIII

STAGGERING SUNDAY

BUT TO brighten up Sundays could confront society with an even worse dilemma. Already Gallup Poll figures show that 15 people in every hundred are at work on Sundays; to increase the available facilities would mean work for even greater numbers. This is one of the basic arguments of the Lord's Day Observance Society: Sunday can never be a secular holiday for *everyone*. If demands for brighter Sundays are met, this will develop into a day in which half the population works to entertain the other half. What is the answer?

We asked people how they would feel about working on Sunday and having a day off during the week instead, About a quarter said they would welcome this arrangement; with the addition of those – less enthusiastic – who 'wouldn't mind,' there are nearly as many in favour of the system as against it. Youth, moreover, is more prone to enthusiasm over the idea than older people.

What are the arguments on either side? One source of feeling against staggered Sundays, often met, is of course rooted in the religious objections. An example of this is the association, present even amongst the non-religious, of Sunday with rest and 'difference.' A 33-year-old working man, for instance, says:

> 'Although I don't go to church, I've an ingrained feeling, stupid perhaps, that on Sundays you shouldn't work.'

Much of this feeling, of course, may be a matter of habit – but it is no less strong for all that:

> 'I don't think I should care for working on Sundays. It would sort of put everything out of gear, routine would be messed up.'
>
> Man, unemployed, cook, 35.

And some insist that Sunday is somehow 'different', even if they do work. Staggered Sundays would forfeit the pleasure of Sunday, a landmark in the week:

MEET YOURSELF ON SUNDAY

'I worked on Sundays all through the war. At first it was strange, but somehow there was always a slight difference to indicate it was Sunday, like crumpets for tea in the mess. But I shouldn't like it in civilian life.'

Manageress, 26.

Many people would be sorry to lose Sunday, which whether religiously or not is different to the rest of the week; they would regret this awareness that most families are enjoying a special day, the crumpets for tea, the national break from routine – in

so far, of course, as it remains a *national* break, and so long as the crumpets are there to enjoy, in whatever form they are desired. And part and parcel of this loss of the sense of a collective holiday would be the parallel forfeiture of the family day. Many of the younger school children quoted in preceding pages enjoyed Sunday because their entire family was there – and many grown up people would dislike Sunday work in as much as it made for loneliness; there would be no day left on which most of one's

STAGGERING SUNDAY

friends and relations were fairly sure to be available. A 66 year-old road sweeper, for instance, who dislikes Sundays ('I'd sooner work, it's no benefit to me to loll about and be lazy'), dislikes the thought of a week-day holiday just as much:

> 'I wouldn't want it at all, it would be worse than a Sunday, it would mean being out of contact with everyone. If I was in the country, yes, out in the land where you can get better absorbed.'

Whether the reasoning on the other side is equally weighty it is not for us to judge. The strongest argument is perhaps the suggestion that better holiday facilities would result from staggering the weekly day off. A 57-year-old retired tea-planter, for instance, would welcome this:

> 'I'd prefer a week-day off, you could find something to do. I'm damned if I know what there is to do on a Sunday in this country.'

A housewife:

> 'I would like that. I'd rather have it. You get so bored with Sundays.'

The opinion of a transport worker, at second hand:

> 'My brother – he's a transport worker – prefers to work on Sundays. He says there's more entertainment in the week.'

And a young woman, analytical chemist:

> 'I should like to be able to work on Sundays often, but not always. Most of the waiters at Lyons prefer working on Sundays – but they won't work on Saturdays because of the football.'

Is a secular world to replace Sunday work objections with Saturday taboos? Resentment at having to work on Saturday afternoon might be lessened by football matches through the week. The possibly unpleasant effect on a minority, of enforced work at a time when the rest of the world is on holiday, could provide another argument for the staggered Sunday. Having the whole family on holiday at the same time just makes hard work for the housewife.

Staggered Sundays would mean better holiday facilities for the day off, less rush and crowd, as well as the elimination of one

MEET YOURSELF ON SUNDAY

empty day in seven. It would avoid the possible injustice of a lonely minority working on a day that everyone else has off, and it would ease a back-breaking day for the housewife. To balance these advantages it would forfeit the single 'different' restful day, marking off the end of the week, associated for some with pleasant relaxation – for others with religious satisfaction; it would lose all that is involved in the conception of the Lord's Day and it would entail a certain amount of holiday loneliness for those who, off on Tuesdays, find their friends are only free on Mondays or Wednesdays. It would mean a break away from tradition, habit and association. Both Sabbatarians and the advocates of 'staggering' can present a convincing picture of what may be at stake, if their demands are not fulfilled. Which side has the most popular support?

At the moment the balance is fairly evenly weighted, but our material suggests that it is the desire for brighter Sundays which is on the increase, and which, given encouragement and the assurance of social approval, may sooner or later develop at the expense of the older restrictions of the Sabbath. A situation which at the moment is the cause of only minor and often unacknowledged rankling and discontent could before long become relatively explosive. A popular move for brighter Sundays may soon be in the news.